Safety Smart

Primary

Teaching Responsibility for Personal and Home Safety

by Susan Julio
contributing editor: Dr. Linda Karges-Bone
story editor: Nan Ryan

illustrated by Gary Mohrman

Teaching & Learning Company
1204 Buchanan St., P.O. Box 10
Carthage, IL 62321

Cover photo by Phil Bellis
Maxwell & Bellis Photographers, Quincy IL

Copyright © 1995, Teaching & Learning Company

ISBN No. 1-57310-015-3

Printing No. 9876543

Teaching & Learning Company
1204 Buchanan St., P.O. Box 10
Carthage, IL 62321

This book belongs to

_____

Table of Contents

Dear Teacher or Parent,

The world is an exciting place to young children, full of possibilities and problems as well. As children explore their homes, communities, schools, and even venture out to recreational sites and family trips, the possibilities and problems grow. We anticipate that children will have pleasant, and therefore safe experiences, but life isn't always so agreeable or predictable. Children must be prepared to deal with emergencies, large and small. *Safety Smart* has been designed to offer children in grades K-3 a simple, developmentally appropriate overview of more than a dozen different life experiences involving personal or family safety. The stories depict young children faced with realistic situations and authentic problems. Enrichment activities provide both a cognitive and social framework for dealing with the safety issues introduced in the stories. Key vocabulary for each story encourages language fluency and offers teachers the opportunity to integrate the *Safety Smart* units into other areas of the curriculum. Finally, the choice of either a traditional test or an authentic assessment gives children and teachers a complete evaluation of how much has been learned and applied to issues of safety.

Today, safety issues continue to shift as our society changes. For example, growing numbers of youngsters have taken on responsibilities as "latch key" kids, coming home to wait for parents who are still at work. In other situations, divorce and separation are more frequent today than ever before and place young children in situations with adults whom they do not know and may not yet trust. How do these children deal with issues of personal body safety? Though it is uncomfortable for adults to recognize, most cases (over 80%) of sexual abuse involve someone that the child knows, such as a mother's boyfriend or date. Finally, as families have become more transient, children may not have grandparents, aunts or even close family friends to turn to in stressful or dangerous situations. They must become capable and resourceful, while retaining their sense of dignity and fun.

Safety Smart offers a child-centered, hands-on, story-centered perspective on safety education. This curriculum resource should become part of a larger, holistic approach to health, safety and social studies in the primary school. The portfolio suggestions can accommodate a variety of writing experiences, class projects, community resources, drug education, crime education and health education materials. Helping young children move beyond their natural egocentric view of the world, into a healthy, responsible view of how they can be safe in a busy, sometimes dangerous environment, is a challenge for parents and teachers. It is delightful to watch youngsters grasp new skills and confidence and to know that they are as safe as we can make them.

Dear Parents,

Keeping young children safe is a priority at home and at school. So we are pleased to introduce a unit of study on personal and home safety, called *Safety Smart*. The children will hear and read stories about young children who deal with real-life safety situations and learn the right way to stay safe in an emergency. The unit covers important issues such as bicycle safety, being lost in the neighborhood, staying home alone, water safety, choosing to avoid harmful substances such as alcohol and cigarettes and personal body safety. The stories are simple and sensitive, not frightening; but they carry important messages. Afterwards, we will learn songs, rules, routines and information about being and staying safe. Perhaps you have a story or experience to share with the children. A rescue? A lesson learned? Talk with me about ways that you might be a part of our *Safety Smart* initiative. Together, we can help the children to learn that safety can be a choice and a challenge, not a matter of luck.

Safely yours,

Teacher

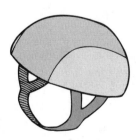

Hints on Using Key Vocabulary

In each chapter of *Safety Smart*, a list of key vocabulary, printed on a large "key," is included for your use. Key vocabulary can be a useful tool for instruction in the primary grades, because it increases both verbal fluency and flexibility. As we know, language is the canvas on which young children paint their experiences. We need to offer them a rich and varied palette with which they can make sense of new experiences and situations. To that end, you might use the key vocabulary to:

- Extend journal writing activities
- Create your own "big books"
- Write sentence strip captions for artwork
- Enrich or take the place of weekly spelling words
- Make posters about safety hints and rules
- Design individual glossaries for the class
- Complete the vocabulary activities provided in the units
- Make your own word finds or crossword puzzles
- Play word games or charades
- Work with language-delayed students to increase expressive and receptive language

A Word About Assessment

Although this book is about instruction, specifically instruction in a home and personal safety curriculum, the connection to assessment is critical. We assess for two reasons: to find out if the children have learned, that is, can apply the material to real life, and also to discern the success of our teaching. For these two reasons the *Safety Smart* curriculum employs two kinds of assessment: traditional tests and authentic assessment tasks. Teachers may select one or both assessments for each chapter and find out a great deal of vital information about the instruction and application of the material.

Grading and Reporting Performance

The traditional tests can be evaluated using a standard numerical point system, but the authentic tasks should be assessed using the rubric and checklist provided in the next section.

What About Portfolio Assessment?

In many schools, portfolios of student work have become popular and important. The tests, tasks and other products that children produce during this unit can be saved in a portfolio. If you like, create a unit-based portfolio on safety issues, but remember that *Safety Smart* is not a stand-alone curriculum for safety. Think of it as part of a larger, more broad "health issues" or social studies program, in which you might include dental health, nutrition, community studies and study of weather-related safety issues, such as floods, fires and storms. More importantly, remember that assessment is a gradual, careful process. Pencil and paper tests only tell part of the story. With young children, their emerging language and problem-solving skills demand a conversational, observational approach to assessment. Observe at the block center, the housekeeping center and as the children play with puppets and dolls. Have they applied the important material outlined in *Safety Smart*? A better question to ask: "Are the children becoming 'safety smart'?"

Class Roster for

Student	Getting Lost	Alone in the House	Personal Body Safety

Teacher may use checks, stars, stickers or stamps to fill in the blanks.

X

Safety Smart

Substance Abuse	Lost in the Woods	Water Safety	Car Safety	Bike Safety

Checklist for Safety Smart K-3

Name: _____   Date: _____

Skill Description of Child's Ability	Level of Competency 1 . . . 2 . . . 3 . . . 4 . . . 5 novice independent
Defines and gives examples of childhood safety issues	
Describes how adults can assist in emergencies	
Can identify emergency helpers and tools, such as 911, first aid kit, flotation devices.	
Verbally describes the steps to take in various safety-related situations	
Demonstrates confidence in his/her ability to handle stressful situations	
Role-plays safety procedures using correct vocabulary and procedures	
Understands the difference between real and make believe in safety-related situations	
Demonstrates creativity and maturity (age appropriate) in finding solutions for safety-related problems	

Cover Art for a Safety Smart Portfolio

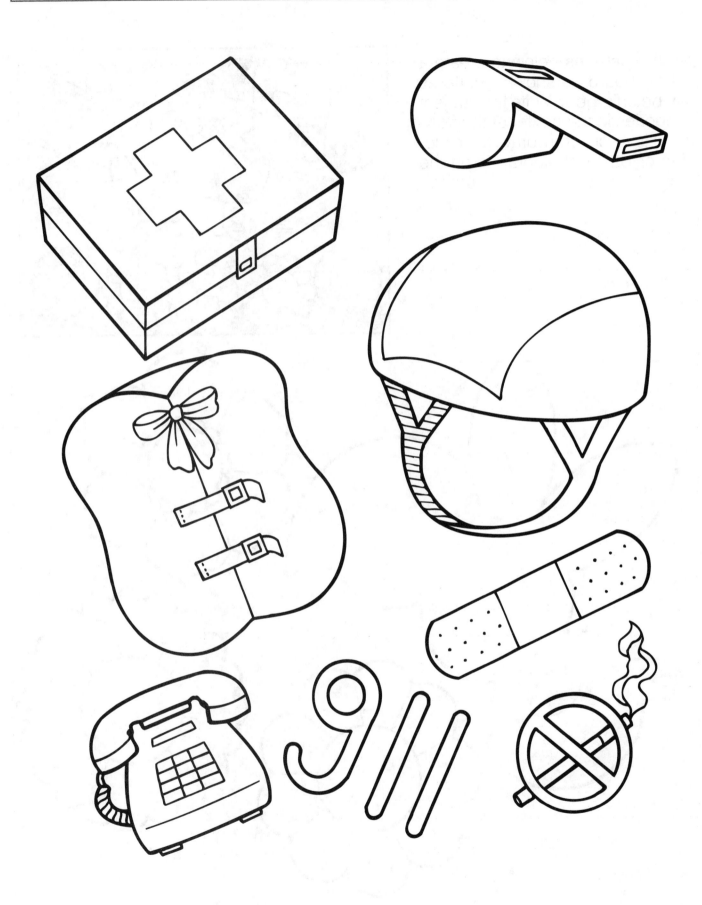

Bulletin Board Patterns

Use the patterns below to create a bulletin board as shown. Patterns may be enlarged. Write the subject categories in the center of the flowers. Have children draw their pictures or paste photographs on the bees.

Chapter 1

Lost in the Neighborhood

Feeling Safe Means Knowing How to Find Your Way Home

Note to Teachers: There are two chapters in *Safety Smart* about the issue of "getting lost." This is developmentally appropriate because young children have not fully formed their senses of time, place and direction. Getting lost in the neighborhood has special dangers: traffic, accidents and possible abduction by a stranger. Therefore it is critical to stress awareness and "staying put," so that the lost can quickly be found.

One sunny afternoon Alex decided to go to the park. He had been there before with his mother and big brother, Tommy, and thought he knew the way.

Alex's mother was busy fixing dinner, so he did not stop to tell her where he was going. I'll be back before she even notices I am gone, he thought, as he slipped out the front door.

Lost in the Neighborhood

He skipped up the sidewalk, eager to get to the park. He passed one street, then another. All these streets look the same, he thought. Alex didn't know which one led to the park.

Suddenly he saw Jason, the school bully, coming his way. Jason was 10 and liked to pick on younger kids. "Hey you," shouted Jason, looking straight at Alex. "Who told you that you could walk on my end of the street, you little pip squeak?"

"I am not a pip squeak, you big old ape," answered Alex.

"I'll teach you to call me an ape," yelled Jason, starting towards Alex.

Without looking, Alex ran across the street and into an alley. It was dark and creepy and had a funny smell. He ran until he came to the other end where it was sunny. He was glad to be back in the light.

This part of town looked familiar. There were the stores where his mother shopped and the big high school that Tommy attended. But there was no park. I wonder how I can get to the park, he thought. I wonder how I can get home?

Alex was lost. He started walking slowly, wondering what to do. He came to a small, dingy house. An old dog was asleep on the porch. Maybe I can call my mother from this house, thought Alex. He was glad he knew his telephone number.

Alex walked up a narrow path to the front door. The dog looked up. Alex stopped and held out his hand. "Here, boy, good dog," he said. The dog growled. Alex was scared. He turned and ran out of the yard and across the street. The dog tried to follow but was stopped with a jerk. Thank goodness, thought Alex, the dog is chained to the steps.

Alex sat down on the curb next to a telephone booth. He didn't know what to do. He felt like crying.

A car pulled up in front of him. "Is there anything wrong?" asked the nice-looking lady in

the car. She smiled at Alex.

"Plenty!" answered Alex. "A big bully tried to fight me, a mean dog tried to bite me, and now I am lost."

"Lost?" said the lady. "Well, get in my car and I will take you home."

Alex was walking slowly to the open car door when he heard his name. "Alex," said a familiar voice. He turned to see Tommy coming towards him, carrying a basketball.

"No thanks, lady," said Alex. "Here comes my brother."

Tommy walked up as the lady sped away. "What are you doing here?" he asked. "Does Mom know where you are?"

Alex shook his head. "I was lost," he said, "but not any more. Will you take me to the park?"

"No," said Tommy. "But I will take you home. We need to talk."

2

After-the-Story Discussion Prompts

With young children, it is a good idea to read each of the stories in *Safety Smart* twice. The first time, simply listen and enjoy the story. The second time, prompt the children to listen for details, and tell them that they will have the opportunity to share in a discussion.

1. Can anyone tell me what happened to Alex?
   - He got lost.
   - He did not listen to his mom.

2. Write the key vocabulary word LOST on a chalkboard or chapter paper. Use big, bold letters. Ask: How did Alex feel when he realized that he was lost?

3. Do you know what to do if you become lost in your neighborhood?
   - Wait for your parents to come.
   - Ask a police officer for help.
   - Look for someone that you know well, such as a family friend or neighbor, but don't leave the area.

4. Is it a good idea to ask a stranger for help?
   - Do not frighten the children, but emphasize the fact that strangers are not friends or family, and we do not ask them for directions or help.

5. Alex should not have gone into the strange house to call home. What could he have done?
   - Used a pay phone.

6. Using hand puppets, role-play the scene in which Alex decides to leave his yard to go to the park. Ask: What could Alex do differently?
   - Accept all responses that demonstrate safe behavior.
   - Prompt children who offer unsafe examples to think about why their decisions might lead to danger or trouble.

After-the-Story Discussion Prompts

7. Ask children: Can you name two neighbors to whom you could go if you were lost or in trouble?

   A neighbor that I trust is _____.

8. Use hand puppets to role-play the scene in which Alex approaches the house that has a growling dog. What could Alex do to be safe in this situation? Did Alex make a good decision when he walked up to this house? Why or why not?

   • Reinforce the fact that this house was a stranger's house. It was not a good decision.

   • Reinforce the idea that Alex should have waited for a family member or police officer to find him.

9. Invite each child to complete this sentence:

   If I were Alex, I would not _____.

10. Invite each child to complete this sentence:

    The next time I go out to play or walk in my neighborhood, I will make sure that I _____.

Enrichment

Invite a representative from the telephone company to bring in a model pay phone and demonstrate how to dial 0 or 911 in an emergency.

4

Name _____

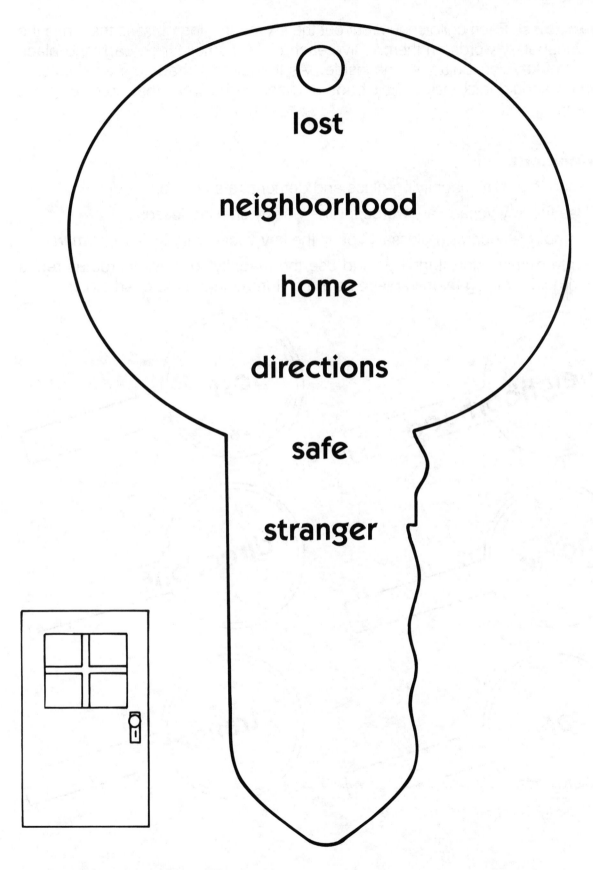

lost

neighborhood

home

directions

safe

stranger

It's in the Bag!

Directions: Each child should cut out the six magnifying glasses that have the key vocabulary words on them. Give each child a small lunch bag, and place the set of key vocabulary words inside. As the teacher reads the words aloud, children should look inside their bags and select the word that completes the sentence.

Enrichment

1. Bring in a real magnifying glass and demonstrate its use.
2. Use the key vocabulary words for the weekly spelling lesson.
3. Compile a separate "glossary" of all the key vocabulary in *Safety Smart*.
4. Write a chart story together, and use the magnifying glass words as rebus words, by gluing them in place as the children dictate the chart story.

Name _____

Lost and Found	Lost: Neighborhood

Directions: Finish each sentence by selecting a key vocabulary word from your bag. Put the words back in after you finish, because they will be used more than one time. Listen carefully.

1. The place where you live is called your ____HOME____.

2. Being free from danger or harm means feeling ____SAFE____.

3. Someone whom you do not know or whom you do not know very well is called a ____STRANGER____.

4. The streets and houses and people near your home make up your ____NEIGHBORHOOD____.

5. To find your way around your neighborhood or back to your home, you must follow ____DIRECTIONS____.

6. When you cannot find your way back to your home, you may be ____LOST____.

7. Your neighbors live close to you, but unless you and your parents know them well, they are still ____STRANGER____, and you should not get into a car with them or go into their homes.

8. You should practice walking to your friend's home or to the park or store, by learning to follow ____DIRECTIONS____.

9. If you get ____LOST____, wait for your parents to come get you, or tell a police officer.

10. To stay ____SAFE____, you should never leave the yard without asking your parents' permission.

11. Another way to stay safe is to know the names of your streets and house number and the name of your ____NEIGHBOR____.

A Neighborhood Map

Directions: Here is a map of Alex's neighborhood. Use a red crayon to trace the path Alex took. Use a green crayon to trace the path he should have taken. Where could he have gone for help?

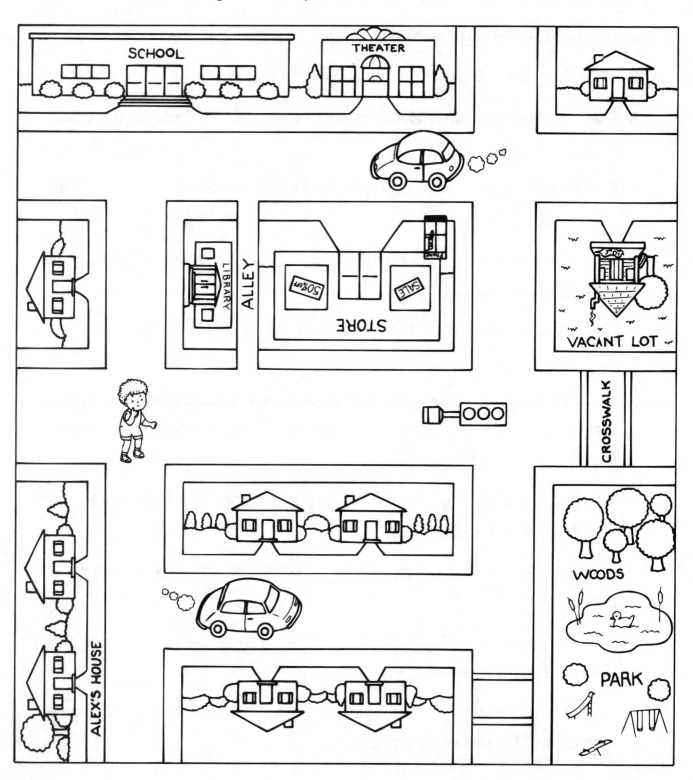

Name _____

Safe House

Directions: Color the picture of the house. Write your name, address and telephone number on the lines. Cut the house out and put it on the bulletin board. Practice saying your name, address and phone number. When you can tell your teacher all of this information without peeking, take your house home!

Note to Teachers: Give children time each day to study their "safe houses" and invite the children to tell you their personal information when they are ready. These houses can then be taken home or placed in the child's portfolio.

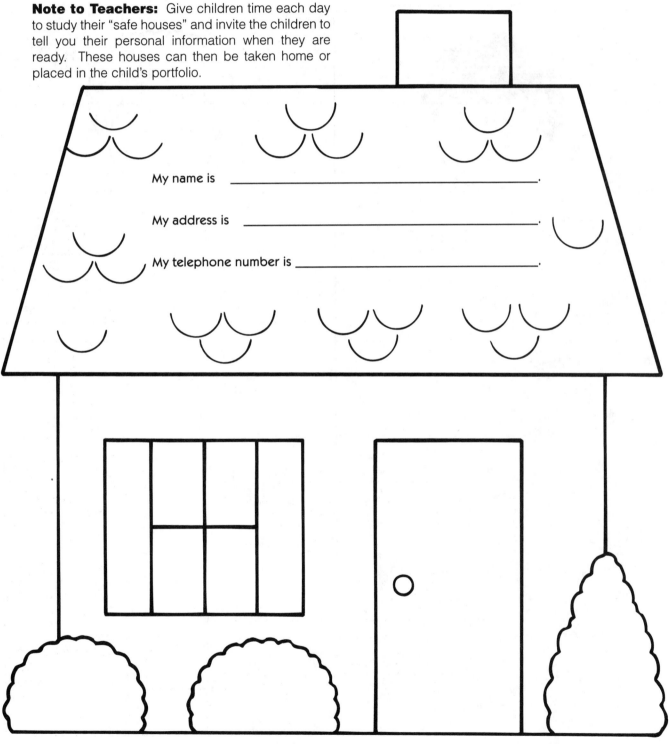

My name is _____.

My address is _____.

My telephone number is _____.

Lost: Neighborhood

Activity

Neighborhood Walk

Directions: Find pictures in magazines or draw your own to show something you should do on a neighborhood walk. Place these under the happy face. Now cut out magazine pictures or draw a scene showing something you should NOT do. Place these under the sad face. Paste or tape your pictures in place.

Name _____

Color the picture.

Name _____

Mapping My Neighborhood

With your family, take a walk through your neighborhood to gather facts for a neighborhood map. Talk to your family about creating your map. Use the list below to help get organized. Then use the stamps on this page to create a map of your neighborhood. Use as many or as few of the stamps as you need. You may also draw pictures on your map. Ask Mom or Dad to label the streets on your map.

1. Decide how large an area you want to include on the map. Set boundaries.

2. Mark off and label streets, neighbor's houses, public buildings and notable landmarks. (You can use the cut-outs provided in addition to your own pictures.)

3. Indicate stop signs and traffic lights.

4. Make red Xs on any dangerous sections of town, such as alleys, fields and woods. Avoid these places!

5. Indicate all telephone booths.

6. Mark houses or areas where dogs are known to be.

7. Put a star on each house or building that can be used as a checkpoint. (For instance, if you cross Elm Street and see trouble, run into Taylor's Drugstore. If you're past Elm Street, go to Oak Elementary School. Once there, find someone who works there and call for help.

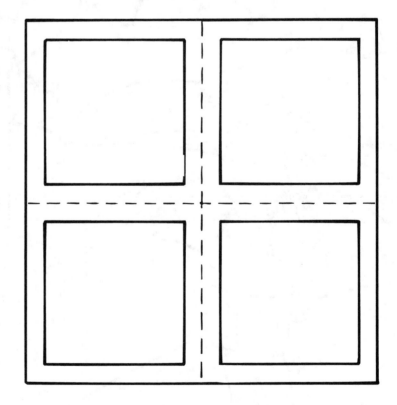

Checking the Story

Directions: Using the six frames below, draw a cartoon that shows Alex from the story, or you, making a safe decision after becoming lost in the neighborhood.

Lost in the Neighborhood

Directions: Read each decision or listen as your teacher reads them aloud. Underline the good decisions with a green crayon. If the decision is a bad one, underline it with a red crayon.

- Each child will need a green crayon and a red crayon.
- Do this in groups of three to five so that you can monitor progress.

1. If you get lost, find an adult and tell him that you are lost.

2. If your mom or dad are busy, it is okay to tell your brother or sister that you are going outside to the park or store.

3. When a growling dog comes near you, hit it with a stick.

4. It is important to know your address and telephone number.

5. If you are lost and see a pay telephone, dial 0 or 911 and someone will tell you what to do.

6. If you get lost in the neighborhood, sit down in a safe place and wait for a member of your family.

7. If you get lost in the neighborhood, start walking and see if you recognize any streets.

8. It is a good idea to talk with your family about which neighbors are also friends and whom you can ask for help if you get lost or in trouble.

Chapter 2

Alone in the House

Note to Teachers: With 55% of mothers in the workforce and 61% of children growing up in single-parent homes–it is likely that many of your students will spend time at home alone.

Ryan carefully felt the house key on the string around his neck. Today would be his first time to come home from school to an empty house. Usually, his mother was there waiting for him, but today, she had some important errands.

"I don't like the idea of leaving you alone," his mother had told him, "but it is only for an hour." She and Ryan had sat down on the sofa. "Let's talk about some things you should know when you are home alone," she had said.

Alone in the House

Ryan took the key from around his neck and put it into the lock of the front door. He walked inside. The house seemed quiet and empty. Ryan locked the door behind him. He felt lonely. Well, Mom will be home soon, he thought. I'll just read one of my books until she gets back.

He curled up on the sofa with one of his favorite stories. The book was so exciting he soon forgot he was alone. Just then, he heard someone knocking at the door. His mother had told him it was very important never to let anyone know that you are alone. "If someone comes to the door," she had said, "you can either not answer it and pretend no one is home, or ask who it is before you open it. If it is a stranger, or someone you don't know well, never open the door."

When they finished talking, Ryan left for school. All day he thought about what his mother had said. Staying home alone was a big responsibility, and he wanted to do a good job. Now school was over. Ryan walked up the stairs to the front door of his house.

He checked the doors and windows to make sure they were still locked and looked to see if anything was different, just like his mother had told him. "A burglar could have broken in the house while we were gone," she had said.

The thought that a stranger could be inside was scary, but Ryan knew he could go next door to Mr. McNally's house and call the police. They would come and check the house to make sure it was safe.

TLC10015 Copyright © Teaching & Learning Company, Carthage, IL 62321

Alone in the House

"I'm a salesman," the voice answered. "I would like to show you some magazines."

Ryan chose his words carefully. "My mother can't come to the door just now. She is busy."

"Okay, kid," said the voice. "Tell her I'll try again another day. Thanks."

Ryan heard footsteps going away. He picked up his book and started to read. The phone rang. Ryan knew what to do. "Hello," he said.

"Who is this?" a man's voice asked.

"Who did you want to speak to?" Ryan asked. I am not going to tell a stranger my name, he thought.

"Is your mother home? I have a message for her," said the voice.

"She can't come to the phone right now, but I will take a message," Ryan answered. He carefully wrote down the man's name, telephone number and the message. "She will probably call you back in a few minutes," Ryan said. He left the message by the phone where his mother would be sure to see it.

Ryan looked at the clock. She should be home soon, he thought. Then Ryan heard the clock ticking. He had never paid attention to the sound before and was surprised how loud it was. I'm glad I know what makes the noise, he laughed to himself.

I remember Mom said if I heard a sound and didn't know what it was, to call Mr. McNally. I guess he is my safety checker. It was nice to know that there was someone to help if needed.

Then Ryan heard a new noise, but that one was easy to figure out. His stomach was growling. Ryan realized how hungry he was. He went to the kitchen and took the cold snack and drink that his mother had left for him out of the refrigerator. She had said not to use any kitchen appliances, like the oven or microwave, because it could be dangerous.

As Ryan bit into the sandwich he heard a key turn in the front door. His mother walked in. How glad he was to see her.

"How did it go?" she asked, bending to give him a kiss.

Ryan smiled. He knew his mother would be proud of him.

After-the-Story Discussion Prompts

Sometimes children stay at home for a few hours by themselves, when their parents have to be at work or when they have an important errand, like Ryan's mother did. Can you think of a time when you might have to stay at home by yourself or with a brother or sister?

- Accept all responses.

1. In the story, Ryan did several safety smart things. Can you name them?

- Keeping doors and windows locked
- Taking a message on the telephone
- Not opening the door to a stranger
- Eating a cold snack instead of touching appliances
- Thinking about calling his "safety checker"

2. Do you think any one of the rules is more important than others?

Listen to responses. Then make a chart of "What might happen if . . . " to demonstrate how each rule is important.

3. Why do you think it is a good idea to have a "safety checker"? How do you get a safety checker?

- To help you feel safe
- To get help quickly
- Your parents select a safety checker

4. Can you name a safety checker for your family?

5. Did Ryan make good decisions while he was at home alone?

18

6. Can you think of other ways to be safely home alone?

7. If something really scary had happened to Ryan, what could he do? Call 911.
   - Call the police.
   - Go to the safety checker's house.
   - Call his parents at work.

8. What should Ryan do if a fire starts at his house while he is at home alone?
   - There is only one answer: leave the house immediately.

9. What if Ryan felt sick while he was at home alone? Is it okay to take some medicine?
   - It is never okay to take medicine by yourself, even if it is your medicine.
   - If you feel really sick, call your parents, your safety checker or 911.

10. Can you name some wise choices of things to do when you are at home alone?

    Accept all responses that are safe, simple and do not require materials such as scissors, tools or chemicals.

    - Read a book.
    - Do homework.
    - Clean your room.
    - Play a board game.
    - Do chores.
    - Color pictures.
    - Play computer games (with permission).
    - Write a note to a friend or relative.
    - Play with your pet; feed your pet.
    - Look at a magazine.
    - Study for your spelling test.
    - Write a poem or story.

Safety Is the Key

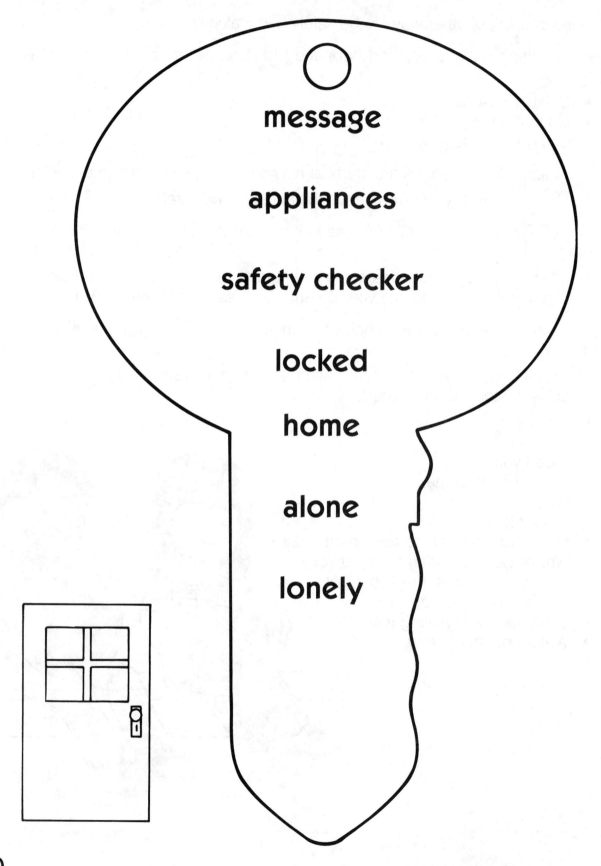

message

appliances

safety checker

locked

home

alone

lonely

Safety Lock Up!

Directions: Match each key phrase to the right vocabulary word by coloring the matching locks and keys the same color.

Never tell anyone you are

_____.

1

If something frightens you when you are alone, call your _____.

2

Always keep the doors and windows _____ when you are at home alone.

3

If you are at home alone, eat a cold snack, and do not touch _____, like the stove or microwave oven.

4

When you are at home alone, it is okay if you feel

_____.

5

If the telephone rings when you are at home alone, always take a _____. Never say that your parents are not at home.

6

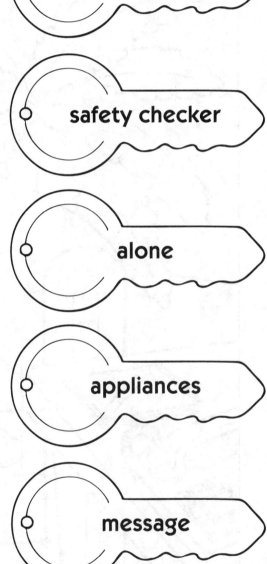

locked

safety checker

alone

appliances

message

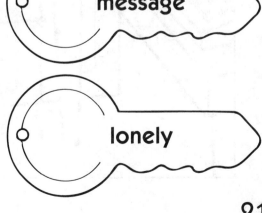

lonely

Name _____

Alone and Safe

Color the picture.

Alone in the House

Directions: Cut out the pictures at the bottom of the next page. Glue each picture in the correct square.

One day Ryan had to come [ ] alone. He had a

[ ] tied on a string. Before going in, he checked to make

sure the [ ] and [ ] were locked.

Then he opened the [ ], went inside and locked it again.

Ryan read a [ ]. He heard a knock at the [ ].

"Who's there?" Ryan asked. It was a salesman. He

wanted to sell [ ]. Ryan did not open the [ ].

The salesman would have to come back later. Then the

[ ] rang. Ryan picked it up. The person on the

telephone wanted to speak to Ryan's mother. "My mother can't

Alone at Home

Activity

Alone in the House

come to the [   ] right now," Ryan said. He took a message.

He did not say that he was [   ] alone! Ryan heard the sound

of a ticking [   ] . He knew what it was. It did not frighten

him. He knew he could call his [   ] if it did. Ryan felt hungry.

He went into the kitchen and took out the [   ] his mother

made him. He would not use any [   ] that might hurt him.

Finally, his [   ] came [   ] . She was very proud of him!

Telephone Safety Memo Pad

Directions: Learning how to answer the telephone in a polite manner that also maintains home security and safety is an important skill.

- Bring in a real telephone and practice answering the telephone in a polite and safe manner.

- Use the response dialogue on the following page to help you with "practice calls."

- Create individual Telephone Safety Memo Pads by reproducing the telephone pattern on construction paper (front and back) and placing several sheets of plain or lined paper in between. Staple the memo pads at the corner. The children may take them home when they have demonstrated the ability to answer the telephone in a polite and safe manner.

Knock, Knock, Who's There?

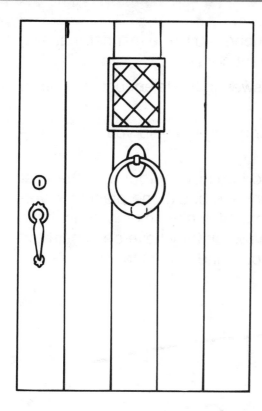

Directions: Children can use puppets or role-play the scenes themselves. Encourage children to use the key vocabulary during these scenes.

To the Teacher: Read each scene aloud, and then ask for volunteers to role-play an appropriate response while pretending that they are "home alone."

Scene 1: "Knock, knock, who's there?" It is a delivery person with a big, important-looking package. What should you do?

- Do not answer the door. They will leave it on the step or leave a note for your parents.

Scene 2: "Knock, knock, who's there?" It is your grandmother."

- It is okay to answer the door to a relative, unless your family have told you *not* to allow a particular person in. But be certain that it *is* your relative before opening the door.

Scene 3: "Knock, knock, who's there?" It is the man who fixes the cable television. He says that your mom said he could come in.

- Do not open the door to anyone, unless your mom has called you and told you to expect someone specific. Then you should ask them to show you their identification card through the window.

Scene 4: "Ring, ring, who's there?" You are staying at your grandma's. A lady who says she is your grandma's friend from work wants to know if your grandma is home. What do you say?

- My grandma will call you back in a few minutes. Can I take a message?
- Don't answer the phone. Let the answering machine pick up, if she has one.

Scene 5: "Ring, ring, who's there?" It is a salesperson, wanting to talk to your mother or father. What do you say?

- I'm sorry, but my mom (dad) is busy right now. You might call back later.

Scene 6: "Ring, ring, who's there?" It is your neighbor, wanting to borrow a cup of sugar. What do you say?

- My mom is busy right now, and can't check on the sugar. I'll have her call you right back.

Scene 7: "Ring, ring, who's there?" It is your tee ball coach, wanting to tell you about practice. What do you say?

- I can write that down now, or you might leave a message for my mom or dad to call you back.

Name _____

My Telephone List

Read over this list with your family. Write in important phone numbers. Keep this list by the telephone so you can find them in a hurry.

My telephone number: _____

Family work numbers: _____

My neighbor's name and number: _____

_____

When I take a message, I will write down . . .

1. Who the message is for.
2. Who the message is from. I will ask them to spell their name.
3. What telephone number to call back. I will repeat it to make sure I have written it down correctly.
4. What the message is, if they want to leave one.

In case of an emergency, I will call . . .

Police: _____

Fire: _____

Hospital: _____

or 911

I will tell them my name: _____

My address: _____

My telephone number: _____

I will tell them what the problem is. I will do what they say. I will turn on the outside light until they arrive.

Name _____

House Rules

Directions: Use the outline of the house to fill in at least three important things that you should remember to do if you are home by yourself. You can draw the scenes and then write the "rule" on the clouds above the house.

Alone at Home

Checkpoint

Checking the Rules

Directions: Draw a little ✓ next to the rules that will keep you safe when you are at home alone. Put an X next to the rules that do not keep you safe.

_____ 1. You should not open the door to anyone when you are at home alone.

_____ 2. It is a good idea to fix a hot snack in the microwave oven when you are at home alone.

_____ 3. If someone calls for your mother, you should ask to take a message on your memo pad.

_____ 4. It is okay to invite friends inside to play when you are at home by yourself.

_____ 5. If you become afraid when you are by yourself, it is good to call your safety checker on the telephone or go over to their home, if they live next door.

_____ 6. If a delivery person comes to the door and tells you that it is important that they come inside, you should let them in if they wear a uniform.

_____ 7. It is safe to keep the doors and windows locked when you are at home alone.

Chapter 3

Personal Body Safety

Note to Teachers: Personal body safety is a sensitive issue. However, it is necessary to give young children a sense of ownership, privacy and power over their bodies. They need to recognize danger and to react to threatening situations with a degree of confidence. With this chapter, and "The Choice" (chapter 4), it is a good idea to send home a letter to parents asking them to review the materials and to give their input.

Kelly straightened the curtains on the windows of the new playhouse her daddy had just finished. The house had a small tiny door, a tiny table and two matching chairs. A vase of flowers sat on the table and a picture of Kelly's family hung on the wall. The house was all she had hoped it would be.

Kelly was excited that her favorite aunt was coming to visit today with her new husband. Aunt Leslie had been married a long time to Uncle Peter, but he died last year. Kelly was looking forward to meeting her new uncle, Ed. Aunt Leslie said they were bringing Kelly a surprise.

Personal Body Safety

Kelly heard a car pull into the driveway. She looked out the playhouse door and saw Aunt Leslie and a tall man walking up the sidewalk toward the house. She raced into Aunt Leslie's arms. "Here's my special girl," Aunt Leslie whispered in Kelly's ear.

Kelly smiled at her aunt. "Would you like to meet your new uncle?" Aunt Leslie asked. Kelly nodded. "Ed, I would like you to meet Kelly," she said, slipping her arm through his. "Kelly, this is your Uncle Ed. I know you will be great friends."

Kelly looked into Uncle Ed's eyes. They were a cold blue, not like Uncle Peter's cheerful brown eyes.

"I am glad to meet you, Kelly," Uncle Ed said. "Your aunt has told me a lot about you." He took Kelly's hand and held it. "I understand you have a new playhouse. We have brought you a housewarming gift. Would you like to see it?"

Kelly pulled her hand away. "Yes, please," she answered shyly.

Aunt Leslie put a large package in front of Kelly. "Please open it," she said.

Kelly tore off the wrapping paper. Inside was a box containing a pink tea set.

"Now you can have tea parties in your playhouse," said Uncle Ed.

"Thank you," said Kelly. "The tea set is perfect. May I take it to my playhouse now?" she asked her mother.

"Yes," answered her mother, "but lunch is in half an hour, okay?"

Kelly walked to her playhouse, holding her tea set carefully. She was just setting the pieces on the table when she heard a knock at the door.

"Am I invited?" asked Uncle Ed, poking his head in. Kelly was startled.

"Well, I guess so," she answered.

Uncle Ed looked very large inside the small house. "Guess I'll sit on the floor," he said. "That chair looks too tiny."

Kelly glanced out the window. "Is Aunt Leslie coming, too?" she asked.

Uncle Ed shook his head. "No, she said you and I should spend some time getting to know each other. What's for tea?"

Kelly looked down at the small dishes. It felt funny, being alone in her playhouse with a grown-up man she had just met. "I . . . I guess we could pretend to have cookies and milk," she answered quietly.

"What's the matter, Kelly? Don't you like your Uncle Ed?" he asked, moving closer. "Sit on my lap and I'll tell you a story." Uncle Ed put his hand tightly around Kelly's arm and tried to pull her close.

Personal Body Safety

Uncle Ed left the playhouse and walked to the house. Kelly sat at the table and wiped tears from her eyes. Maybe he was just trying to be nice, she thought. But why am I so frightened and confused, she wondered.

Just then her father opened the playhouse door. "Lunchtime, Kelly. What is taking so long?"

Kelly put her head down on her arms. "Daddy," she said, "I have something I want to tell you." Softly she told him about Uncle Ed. "I'm sorry I wasn't nice to him," she said. "Are you angry?"

Her father picked her up gently and stroked her hair. "Not at you, Kelly. You did the right thing. It's not your fault."

"But I told Uncle Ed's secret," she said.

"You should always tell someone about secrets that make you feel bad," he answered. "Now let's go into the house. You can eat lunch with your mother and Aunt Leslie. I need to talk to Uncle Ed."

"No!" Kelly shouted. "I don't want to. You are holding my arm too tight."

Uncle Ed smiled. "Come on, Kelly. I'm your uncle. It's okay."

Just then they heard Aunt Leslie calling, "Ed! Kelly! Are you back there? It is time for lunch."

"I am going in," Kelly said, starting for the door.

Uncle Ed blocked the way. "Look, Kelly," he said softly, "Aunt Leslie doesn't need to know about this, okay? We'll keep our little tea party a secret, all right?"

"You hurt my arm," Kelly said. "Why shouldn't I tell her?"

Uncle Ed frowned. "Because she wouldn't believe you," he answered. "Besides, I was just playing around, trying to be nice. If I were you, I wouldn't say anything."

After-the-Story Discussion Prompts

When dealing with young children, avoid direct lines of questioning. It may make the children feel like they are being interrogated. Instead, aim for a simple, conversational tone. Begin with something like: "Let's talk about what happened to Kelly," and proceed with the following prompts:

1. Was Kelly excited to have a playhouse? Is it fun to have friends and family to play with?

   - Accept all answers.
   - Talk about the difference between friends and family.
   - Talk about trusting people who have earned your trust. Discuss being friendly but careful around people whom you don't know very well.

2. Why do you think Uncle Ed made Kelly feel "confused"? Is that the same as feeling afraid?

   - Give examples of how it feels when you are confused.
   - Give examples of how it feels when you are afraid.
   - Cite passages from the story that show how Kelly felt when certain things occurred.

3. Did an adult ever make you feel confused or afraid?

   - Be careful to protect privacy during this discussion.
   - Look for general answers here.
   - Be prepared to talk to a child privately if you suspect a problem, and be sure to follow all school district and state guidelines for handling such a referral.
   - Remember, the objective of this lesson is to "teach" children about safety, not to interview them.

4. There are lots of reasons for feeling afraid, but today, we are talking about feeling confused or afraid when someone touches you in a way that makes you feel bad. It is never okay for someone to touch your private parts, the parts that your swimsuit covers. Does everyone understand?

   - Review: Private parts are the area that a child's swimsuit covers.
   - Suggestion: Use a doll to demonstrate where the private parts are.
   - Suggestion: Integrate this lesson with your existing curriculum on personal body safety.
   - Suggestion: Does the Junior League in your city offer the "Kids on the Block" puppet show on personal body safety? Are there other programs available in your area?

5. Only your parents can touch you there (in private places), and that is when they help you to get dressed or take a bath. Other children or other adults should never touch your private parts. (Exception: Health care provider with parents' approval.) What should you do when someone asks to touch you or tries to touch you on a private part?

Responses: Run away.
Yell for help.
Tell them "No!
    Do not touch me,"
    and move away.
Get your teacher.
Get your parent.

6. What if an adult tries to frighten you by saying something mean or asking you to keep something that they did a secret? Then what do you do?

   Responses: Tell them to go away.
   You move away and go to your teacher or parent.
   Don't believe them; they are just trying to frighten you.

7. Nice people don't frighten children. They don't ask children to keep secrets. Remember that your body is private. Nobody has the right to touch you on a private part.

8. What if an adult asks you to go somewhere with them and your parent or teacher has not given you permission? Should you go?

   Responses: It is never okay to go into another room or in a car with an adult or teenager. You should not go into a place alone with a family member, or a family friend, if he or she makes you feel confused or afraid.

9. How did Kelly handle her problem? What would you do if the same thing happened to you?

   • Make a chart of the children's responses to this question. Share the responses with parents during an open house or as part of your newsletter. Let the parents know how important it is that they listen to their children and respond in a loving, calm, manner.

Key Vocabulary

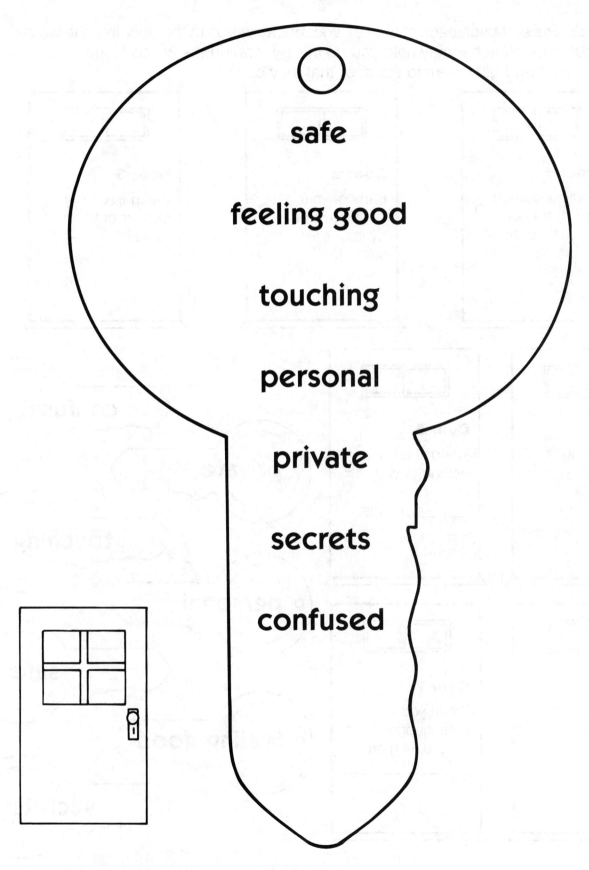

safe

feeling good

touching

personal

private

secrets

confused

Name _____

Open the Doors to Safety

Directions: Match each of the key vocabulary words to the door that the words unlock. Your teacher may help you do this by reading the words aloud. Cut out the "keys" and glue them to the door that they open.

Door 1
Feeling worried or upset about something that you don't understand

Door 2
Parts of your body covered by your swimsuit

Door 3
Being free from danger or harm

Door 4
When you don't tell your parents about something, you are keeping _____.

Door 5
Things that belong to you only are your _____ things.

Door 6
Putting your hands on a person or object

Door 7
When you are safe, happy, secure, you are _____ _____.

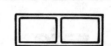

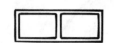

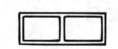

confused

private

touching

personal

safe

feeling good

secrets

Good Touches!

Color the picture.

Personal Safety

Activity

Body Safety Mobile

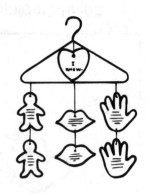

Directions: Cut out the patterns below. Trace and cut out two of each pattern from colored construction paper. Cut out the heart shape and the labels. Glue the labels onto the shapes like this:

about good touches: glue onto one hand shape
about bad touches: glue onto the other hand shape
about good secrets: glue onto one set of lips
about bad secrets: glue onto the other set of lips
how to say "no!":   glue onto one person shape
who to tell.:   glue onto other person shape

Punch a hole in the top of each shape and tie with string to a hanger. Hang in your room.

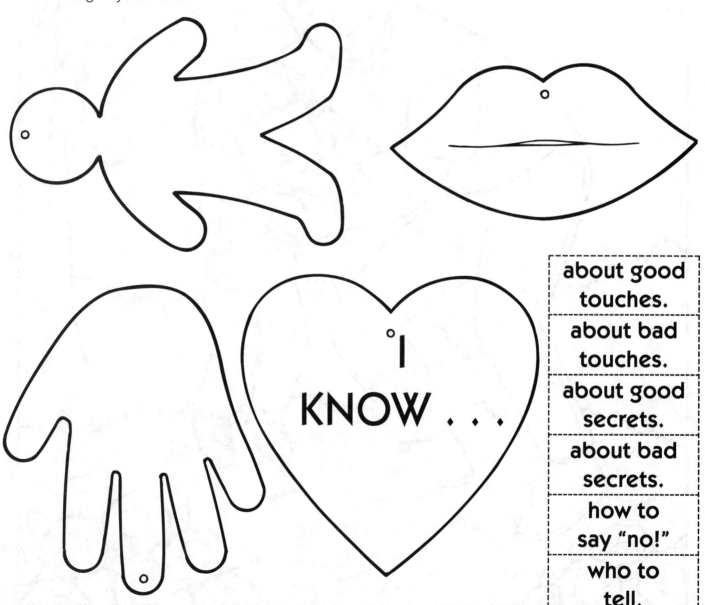

°I

KNOW . . .

about good
touches.

about bad
touches.

about good
secrets.

about bad
secrets.

how to
say "no!"

who to
tell.

40

Name ______________________________

"You Have Rights!"

Personal Safety

Activity

Directions: Draw a picture of yourself in the area below. Show how special you are! Then cut out the "right boxes" below that tell about your rights. Glue them in the four boxes. Put a big red X on the boxes that are not anybody's rights!

A Picture of ______________________

My rights are in these boxes.

1

2

3

4

My body is private!	Bad touches are okay if I don't tell anybody.	Feeling good means feeling safe.
Nobody can touch my private parts.	A baby-sitter can make me keep a bad secret.	I have the right to feel safe.

Personal Safety

Activity

Good Touch, Bad Touch

Step 1: Each child should trace and cut out the shape of his *right hand* on green paper and his *left hand* on red paper. Glue each hand cutout to a craft stick.

Materials: red and green construction paper
glue
pencils
two craft sticks for each child

Step 2: Read the situations aloud, and then ask the children to respond by holding up a "green hand" for YES or a "red hand" for NO. The objective is: Are these good situations or bad situations?

Situations to Consider

1. Your mom's boyfriend touches you in a private place when he is baby-sitting while Mom gets her hair fixed. Good or bad? (Red)
2. Your PE teacher hugs you when you win a race. Good or bad? (Green)
3. A neighbor stares at you and makes you feel afraid. Good or bad? (Red)
4. Good touches make us feel happy. (Green)
5. It is okay to keep a secret from your parents. (Red)
6. Your grandfather wants to show you movies or pictures that make you feel confused or bad. (Red)
7. Your grandfather tells you funny stories. (Green)

Name _____

Personal Body Safety Booklet

Dear Parents,

We have been learning about keeping our bodies safe from unwanted touches or frightening and confusing situations. To help your child make a Personal Body Safety Booklet, follow these directions:

1. Cut booklet pages apart.
2. Make a cover from construction paper cut to size. Staple cover and pages together.
3. Read the pages with your child, filling in the blanks on the last page.
4. Have your child color the pages. Read the book again and talk about it together.

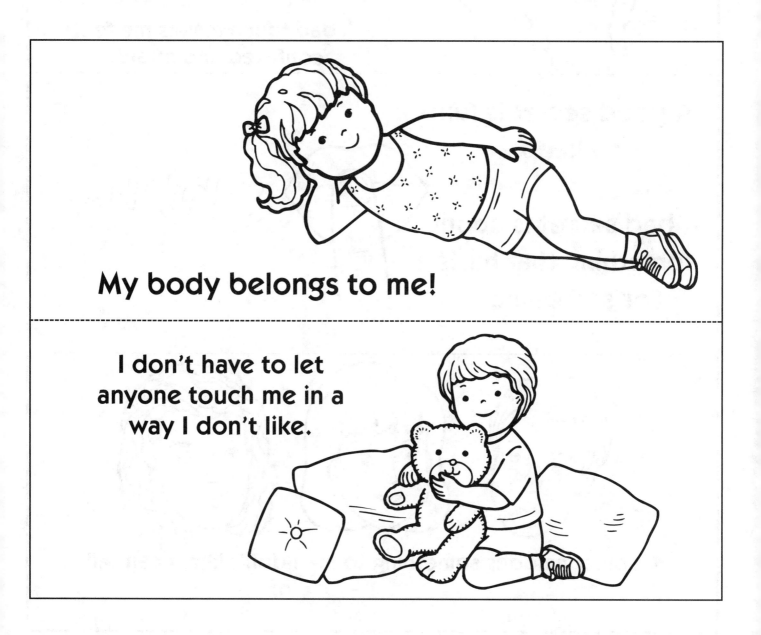

My body belongs to me!

I don't have to let anyone touch me in a way I don't like.

Personal Body Safety Booklet

A good touch makes me feel happy.

A bad touch makes me feel confused and afraid.

A good secret is fun to keep.

A bad secret is about something that hurts or scares me.

Shhh...

If someone does something to me I don't like, I can tell _____, _____ or _____.

44

Hands-On Learning

Directions: On each finger of one "hand" write a response that tells someone "No!" you don't like the way they are touching or treating you. On each finger of the other "hand," write a response that tells about a good touch. The thumb of each hand has been done to help you.

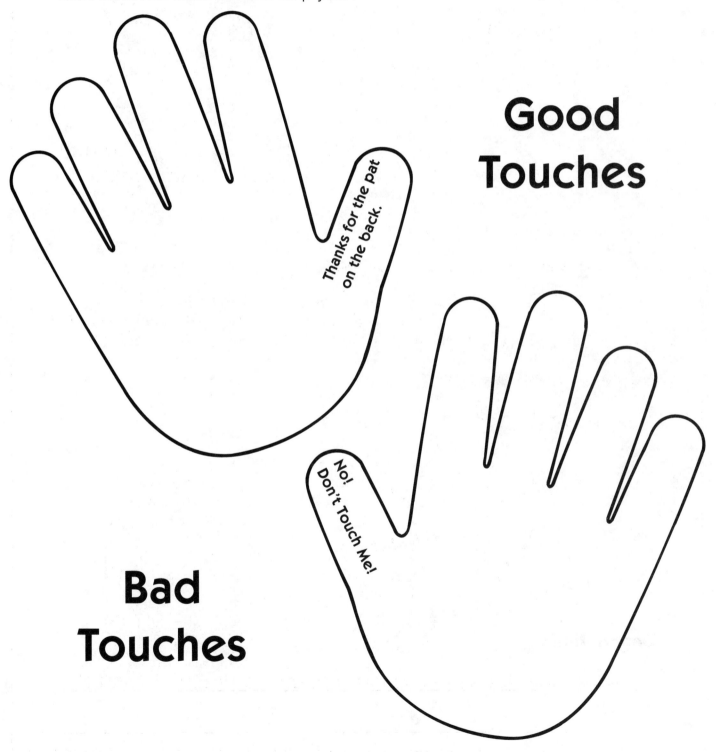

Good Touches

Thanks for the pat on the back.

No! Don't Touch Me!

Bad Touches

Personal Safety

Authentic Assessment

"I Have the Right to Feel Safe!"

Prompt: You are spending the night with your best friend. During the night your friend's dad makes you feel confused or afraid by touching you. Draw a picture that shows what you should do to be safe. Write a sentence on the line below that describes your picture.

Description:

_____

_____

Checking the Rules

Directions: Answer *yes* or *no* to each question. Or draw a or as your teacher reads each question aloud.

1. It is okay for someone to touch you in a way that makes you feel confused or afraid.

    _____

2. Good touches make us feel happy and comfortable.

    _____

3. Keeping a secret from your parents is okay.

    _____

4. Your private parts are covered by your swimsuit.

    _____

5. Your body is private. It belongs to you.

    _____

6. If someone touches you in a bad way, you should move away or tell them to "stop!"

    _____

7. If someone tells you that it is okay to do something that makes you feel confused or afraid, they must be right.

    _____

8. Friends and family members should respect your privacy.

    _____

Chapter 4

The Choice

Note to Teachers: This story can be used with other substance abuse curricula. Drugs are not mentioned in this story, but you can introduce marijuana if it is an issue in the primary schools in your area. The point is to avoid all harmful substances.

Adam bounced his basketball against the school yard blacktop and wiped his forehead with his sleeve. The sun beat down on his head. In a corner of the yard, several older boys huddled against the school's brick wall.

"Hey kid," one of the boys said to Adam, "want to have some fun?"

The Choice

Adam held the ball and stared at the boy. He didn't know him. Better keep away from strangers, he thought. Then he looked closely and saw a smaller figure in the group of boys. It was Taylor, a classmate. Taylor looked up at Adam and smiled. "Hey, come on, Adam, let's have fun," he said.

Adam walked slowly toward the group. He noticed some open cans on the ground, and there was a smell of smoke in the air. Several boys held cigarettes.

"This stuff is cool," said Taylor. "I see my dad drinking beer all the time, and my mom smokes. She says it's not good for her, but she does it anyway. She must like it."

"Want to try some?" asked one of the boys, offering Adam a shiny can. The can felt cool in Adam's hand. He sniffed the liquid inside, but he didn't like the smell.

"I don't think so," he answered, handing the can back.

"Well, at least take a puff on this," said another boy, handing him a lighted cigarette. The smoke made Adam's eyes itch. He began to cough.

"No thanks," he said, backing away. "I know all about that stuff. It is not good for your body."

The Choice

"Oh, a little bit can't hurt you," one of the boys said, laughing. "Besides, the people you see smoking and drinking on TV don't look like they are sick. They look like they are having a good time."

Adam didn't know what to say. He had seen people having a good time drinking and smoking on TV, too.

Taylor walked over to Adam. "Come on," he said. "Let's both try some. You are my friend, aren't you?"

Adam glanced at the shiny cans of beer. They looked cold and refreshing in the hot sun. He was thirsty. He saw the older boys pass the cigarette around. Each took a puff and blew out clouds of smoke.

Adam thought about how strong and healthy he felt. Why, he could ride his bike up the big hill without losing one breath. His body was in tiptop shape. Those boys were crazy!

Adam felt very uncomfortable. Something isn't right about all this, he thought. He knew what to do. Standing up straight, he looked at the older boys. "No thanks," he said, quietly. "I have better things to do with my time." Quickly he turned and walked away.

"Fraidy Cat. What kind of a friend are you?" Taylor shouted to his back.

The older boys laughed. "Aw, let the little baby go home," they said.

Adam didn't care. They could laugh all they wanted. At home that night, he told his parents what had happened.

"Oh, Adam," said his mother. "We are so proud of what you did. And thank you, for telling us what happened."

Adam smiled. He felt good about himself.

1. Can you get a new body, like you can buy a VCR or a bicycle?

   • No, your body is unique. You cannot replace it.

2. In the story, Adam saw some classmates making bad choices about their bodies and health. Can you tell me about these choices?

   • Smoking cigarettes
   • Drinking alcohol

3. Let's talk about the cigarettes first. Why are cigarettes so harmful to your body?

   • Cigarettes make your lungs dirty and weak.
   • Cigarettes can give you serious diseases.
   • Cigarettes make you cough and feel bad.

4. Does a kid look "cool" if he or she smokes cigarettes?

   • No, kids look foolish when they smoke!

5. How about drinking alcohol? Is it a good choice to drink alcohol?

   • No, drinking alcohol is a bad choice.
   • Alcohol makes your body weak and sick.
   • Alcohol hurts your brain. It kills brain cells, and you won't be as smart or quick.

6. What can you drink to make your body strong?

   • Juice, water, milk

7. How did the cigarette smoke make Adam feel?

   • His eyes itched and he coughed.

8. Why didn't Adam walk away right then?

   • Accept all answers.
   • Lead toward: he hadn't made his choice yet.

After-the-Story Discussion Prompts

9. What did Adam think about when he made his choice to walk away?

   • He thought about how strong and healthy his body was. He didn't want to hurt his body.

10. Did Adam worry about what other people thought?

    • No! Adam was a strong person. He wasn't afraid to make good choices.

11. Why did Adam tell his parents about the other boys? Why is it important not to keep secrets from parents?

    • He wanted his parents to be proud of him.
    • His parents could talk to the other boys' parents.
    • It is important to be truthful with our family because they care about us and want to help us.

12. Why did Adam feel good about himself at the end of the story?

    • He made a good choice.
    • He took care of his body.
    • He told his parents what happened, and they were proud of him.

13. What would you do if you were Adam?

    • Accept all answers that lead to healthy choices.

14. Who can help you if you are worried about cigarettes or alcohol or if your friends try them?

    • Parents, teacher, guidance counselor, principal, school nurse, doctor, minister, police officer, etc.

In the primary grades, distinguishing between real and make-believe, fantasy or reality, are critical thinking skills that should be taught and practiced. Lead a class discussion that helps children understand that commercials or TV shows are not glimpses of real life. They are make-believe, feel-good images that are designed to sell products or entertain. Try the following instructional strategies:

1. Make a list of the ways that commercials and TV shows present alcohol.

   • Parties and celebrations
   • People at the beach
   • People making friends
   • Pretty, handsome, smart people drinking alcohol

2. Ask the children: Do these commercials or TV shows ever show people after drinking alcohol, when they

   • get hurt in car accidents
   • get sick or hurt
   • yell at other people
   • make bad decisions

3. Make a list of how actors in movies and television look when they smoke cigarettes.

   • Cool
   • Grown up
   • Exciting

4. Ask the children if these actors show how cigarettes

   • make people sick and die
   • cost a lot of money
   • make you tired and weak
   • give you bad breath and make your clothes smell awful
   • cause burns and fires

5. Encourage the children to make their own list of why they choose not to drink alcohol or use cigarettes.

Key Vocabulary

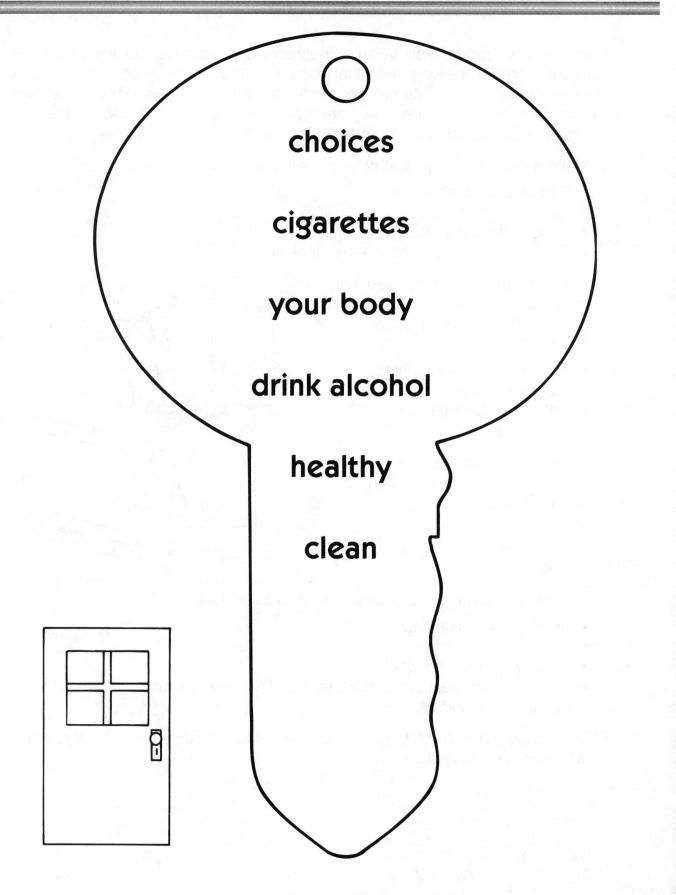

choices

cigarettes

your body

drink alcohol

healthy

clean

Healthy Choices

Directions: Read the definition on each microwave dinner. Then find the "fork" below that has a matching key vocabulary word. Cut out the forks and glue them next to the dinners that they match. Color the forks and dinners.

1. Smoking these can harm your body.

2. It is not healthy for children to have beer or to _____.

3. If you don't smoke, your lungs stay strong and _____.

4. When your body is in good shape, it is _____.

5. You can decide to have a healthy body. You can make good _____.

6. You only have one of these, so take good care of _____.

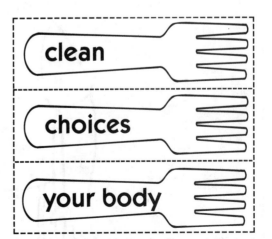

drink alcohol

healthy

cigarettes

clean

choices

your body

Name _____

My Healthy Choices

Color the picture.

Smart Choices

Directions: Look at the picture below. Color the head to look like you. Draw some things inside the body that you could eat or drink to make your body grow strong and healthy.

Name _____

Get the Message?

Directions: What have you learned about taking care of your body? There are things that hurt your body and things that help your body to stay strong and healthy. Design a tee shirt that shows how to stay strong.

Create an Ad

Use this space to create your own ad. Tell why a person should NOT smoke cigarettes or drink alcohol.

Write your slogan on the line and draw a picture to go with it.

Note to Teachers: You may wish to brainstorm slogans as a whole class activity. Children can then choose one slogan to use in their ad.

_____

Name _____

Healthy Food Choices

Helping a child to make good choices about having a healthy body means more than just avoiding harmful substances such as alcohol, cigarettes or drugs. Families can create a healthy lifestyle together by choosing meals and snacks that give energy and build strong minds and bodies. Make out this grocery list with your child, and then go shopping. How many healthy choices can you make together?

 ## Our Healthy Family Grocery List

Green Vegetables

_____

_____

_____

Yellow or Orange Vegetables

_____

_____

_____

Rice and Grains

_____

_____

_____

Dairy Products/Proteins

_____

_____

_____

Beverages

_____

_____

_____

Snacks

_____

_____

_____

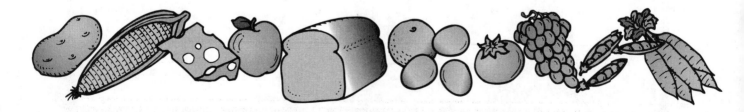

Name ____

Healthy Body Warranty Card

Body Safety

Authentic Assessment

When you buy a new car or a new VCR, it comes with a warranty. This means that the company that sold it to you has to take care of it for a long time, even if it breaks. You have to take care of your body by making healthy choices. Fill in the Healthy Body Warranty Card to show that you know how to take care of your body.

Healthy Body Warranty Card

This healthy body belongs to ________________________________

The birthday of this healthy body is on

____

As the owner of this healthy body, I will do the following things every day:

____

____

____

As the owner of this healthy body, I will not ever do the following things:

____

____

I am proud of my healthy body, and my favorite parts are my

____

____

My signature: ________________________________

Name _____

Taking Care of Your Body

Directions: Place a ✓ by each statement that tells about healthy choices. Place an X by each statement that tells about choices that are not healthy.

_____ 1. Cigarettes can't really hurt you.

_____ 2. People will think you're a baby if you don't try some alcohol.

_____ 3. Eating good foods helps to make your body healthy.

_____ 4. If you smoke cigarettes, you will look cool.

_____ 5. You should do what is right and healthy, no matter what other kids say or do.

_____ 6. TV commercials show the truth about drinking alcohol. It is fun and exciting.

_____ 7. Smart people make careful choices about what they see on TV commercials.

_____ 8. You only have one body, so you should take good care of it.

_____ 9. Cigarettes and alcohol make you feel good.

_____ 10. Smoking and drinking alcohol make your body sick and weak.

Chapter 5

Lost in the Woods

Feeling Safe When You Are Camping or Hiking

Note to Teachers: Remember that young children are egocentric and that their concepts of time and distance are not fully developed. Getting lost on an outing is a real possibility.

Ashley zipped up the jacket of her winter coat. Her parents were busy packing the car with camping gear. Soon they would take down the red tent. The air had gotten colder overnight, and her father was worried about an early snow. Ashley loved camping. She was sorry they had to leave so soon.

Her mother smiled. "Maybe you would like to feed some leftover bread to the birds," she said, handing Ashley a plastic bag. "If it does snow tonight, I bet they would like to have full tummies."

Lost in the Woods

Ashley took the bag and walked towards the woods. "Stay close," called her father. "We should leave soon. I don't like the looks of those clouds."

They seem soft and squishy, thought Ashley, as she looked up at the pretty puffy gray clouds drifting overhead in the dull sky.

Ashley took a slice of bread from the bag and tore it into small pieces. She dropped them on the ground and watched as a few birds flew down from the tree and cautiously picked up the bread in their beaks.

Suddenly she heard a noise. Turning quietly, she saw a flash of brown and tan. A deer! Ashley tried to follow the deer as it darted between trees and bushes. But the faster she ran, the faster the deer ran. Soon it was out of sight. She felt sad. Ashley thought about the deer as she walked through the woods. I wonder where it will go if it snows, she thought. I hope it won't get too cold.

She glanced up at the sky. The gray clouds had gotten thicker. The day seemed darker and colder. She shivered as she put her hands in the pockets of her jacket. I must have run a long way, she thought as she walked. It is taking me a long time to get back. I wonder. I wonder if I am going in the right direction?

64

Lost in the Woods

There was no red tent in sight. She could not hear any familiar sounds. She didn't remember the fallen tree across the path. Ashley started to cry and began to run. "I think I'm lost," she whispered out loud to the woods. "Mommy, Daddy, where are you?" she cried.

Snowflakes drifted down around her. "Oh no," she said. "Don't snow. I am lost, and I am scared. I don't know what to do." No one heard her but the animals in the forest. She tried to think what her father had told her on their last camping trip about getting lost in the woods.

Suddenly she remembered. "Stop," he had told her. "Stop where you are and think. Look around for footprints to show where you have been." Ashley stopped and looked around, but there were no footprints. The snow had covered them.

"See what you have with you," she remembered him saying. Ashley checked her pockets and found a half-eaten granola bar and a small silver whistle. Daddy gave me this whistle to blow if I get lost, thought Ashley. I remember, he said the international distress call is three short blasts. She took a deep breath and blew as hard as she could.

"Tweeeeet! Tweeeeet! Tweeeeet!" The noise cut through the silence of the woods. I am almost too cold to blow, thought Ashley, watching the snow fall. I wonder how I can get warm? Then she remembered. Her daddy had told her to look around for a warm place, like under the branches of a cedar tree or a fallen tree or behind a large boulder. She looked around.

There was a newly fallen tree. She poked between its branches checking for any creatures that might be there and eased herself in among the leaves. She blew the whistle, one-two-three. What if no one hears me, she thought.

Just then she heard her name. She blew her whistle as hard as she could and saw her daddy moving towards her. "Daddy," she cried, climbing out of the branches. "I got lost."

She felt his strong arms lifting her up against his wet cheek. "I am glad I found you," he said softly. "You remembered about the whistle." "Yes," said Ashley proudly. "I remembered everything you told me. Now I am safe."

After-the-Story Discussion Prompts

After reading "Lost in the Woods" lead a teaching discussion about Ashley's experience. Reinforce the key vocabulary: STOP, THINK, LOOK, WAIT, DECIDE!

1. Have you ever been on a camping or hiking trip with your family or a scouting or church group?
   - Accept all answers.
   - Make a chart of places where people go for outdoor recreation: state parks, campgrounds, the woods, the forest, the beach, the mountains.

2. Why is being lost in the woods *different* from being lost in the neighborhood?
   - There will not be other people to ask for help.
   - There are no landmarks, street signs or telephones.
   - There may be danger from animals, poisonous plants, weather, high places, rocks or deep water in the outdoors.

3. If being lost in the woods might be dangerous, why is it important to STOP and THINK before you go any further?
   - People can find you if you stay in one place.
   - You might not get hurt.

4. Why is it a good idea to carry a whistle like Ashley did?
   - The woods are thick and hard to see in, but people can hear a whistle.

5. Who remembers the special way that Ashley blew the whistle?
   - Three short blasts: the international distress signal.

66

6. To *really make a point*, hand out individual whistles and practice the whistle. You may get these donations from a local hardware or discount store. Be sure to ask for elastic wristbands as well.

7. What decisions did Ashley have to make in the story?
   - To go out on the walk by herself (bad decision)
   - To try to retrace her footsteps (good decision)
   - To stop and wait when she realized that her footprints had been covered by snow (good decision)

8. Do you think it is easy to get lost in the woods?
   - Emphasize the fact that this (the woods) is unfamiliar to many children. You need special skills to live outdoors for more than a few hours.

9. What should you keep in your backpack when you camp or hike? Make a class list or go to the "Camping Back-pack," page 77.
   - bottle of water
   - dried fruit, chocolate snacks
   - jacket and hat
   - flashlight
   - whistle
   - flare

10. Asking permission is always a good safety choice. Why do you think kids forget to ask permission? How can you help yourself or others to remember?
    - Kids get excited when they are outdoors.
    - Like Ashley, you can wander away without meaning to.
    - Wear your wristband whistle to help you remember.
    - Stay with a buddy!

Key Vocabulary

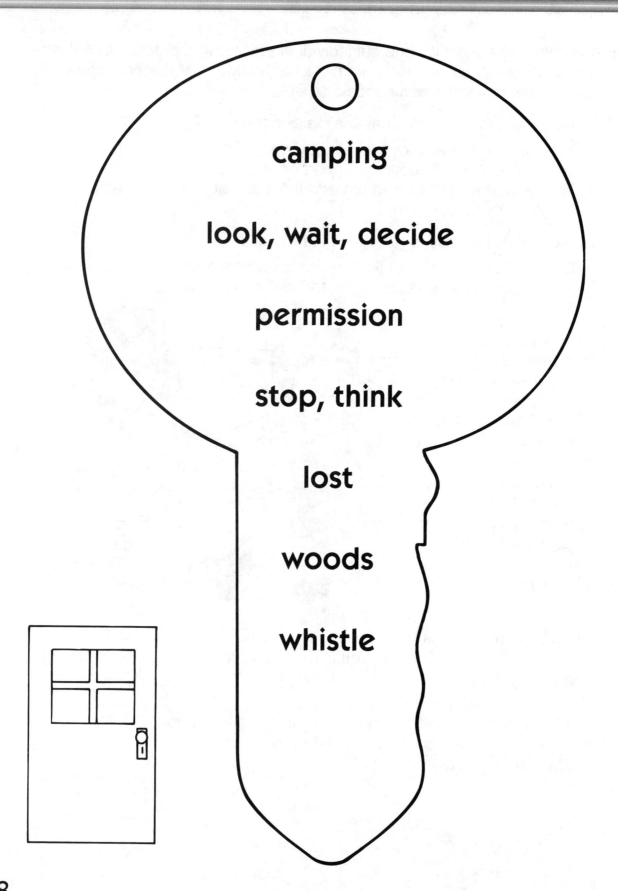

camping

look, wait, decide

permission

stop, think

lost

woods

whistle

Campsite Safety

Directions: Some of the key vocabulary words or phrases are printed on a shape. Say the words. Color the shapes. Cut the shapes out and use them to create a picture of your campsite. You can use green paper for a "woodsy" background or blue paper if you want to camp out at the beach.

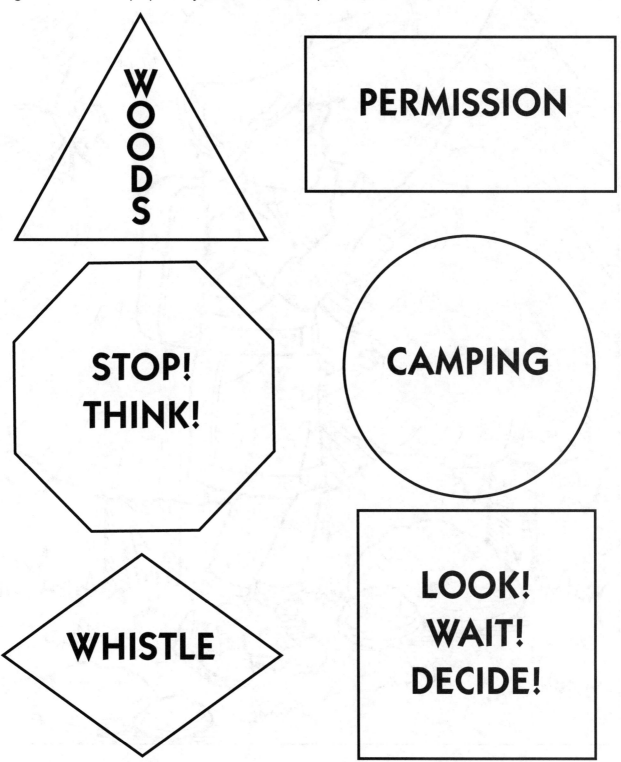

WOODS

PERMISSION

STOP! THINK!

CAMPING

WHISTLE

LOOK! WAIT! DECIDE!

Name _____

Lost: Woodsw

Activity

In the Woods

Color the picture.

70

TLC10015 Copyright © Teaching & Learning Company, Carthage, IL 62321

Name _____

What Happens Next?

Directions: Look at the pictures below. The little girl is lost in the woods. Decide what she should do first. Put a 1 in the box at the top of that picture. Continue numbering each picture until all of them are in order.

Lost: Woods

Activity

Safe in My Tent

Directions: Pretend you are in the woods on a camping trip. Color the tent below. Use your scissors to cut on the dotted line and bend back to make a flap. Glue the tent (don't glue the flap!) to a file folder. Open the flap and draw a picture of yourself inside the tent! Write a sentence about being safe in the woods.

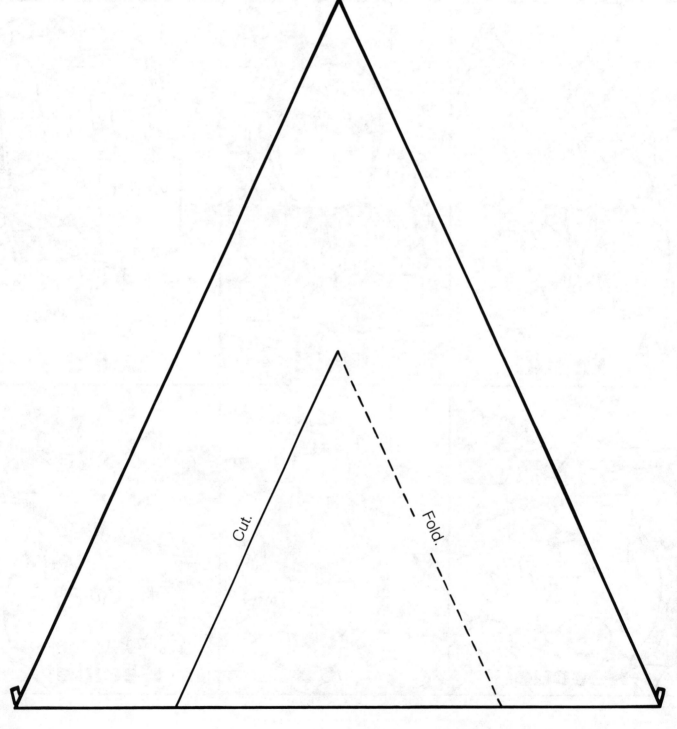

Cut.

Fold.

TLC10015 Copyright © Teaching & Learning Company, Carthage, IL 62321

Act It Out

Directions: Reproduce and cut apart the slips below. Place them in an empty knapsack. Invite the children to take turns choosing a slip and reading the problem out loud. Have them act out how they would solve the problem. (Encourage the students to use classroom items for props if needed–a chair could be a fallen tree, etc.) Have other students play additional roles so everyone can participate.

You are at a campsite with your mom and dad.
You see a pretty butterfly you'd like to catch with your butterfly net.
The butterfly is flying into the woods. What should you do?

You went to a stream to get some water in a bucket for cleaning your camp dishes.
You thought you knew the way back, but now you aren't sure. What should you do? You know your parents are close by; you're just not sure where.

Somehow you have gotten lost in the woods.
You have stopped, but it has started to get dark and cold.
What should you do?

You see a good shelter inside a hollow log.
What should you do first?
How can you make it warmer?

You are snug in your shelter, but you are hungry.
You have a candy bar in your pocket.
What will you do?

You, your parents and your brothers and sisters have gone on a picnic.
Your little sister has wandered off into the woods.
What should you do?

Your best friend says he knows where there's a
good place to catch frogs in the woods behind your house.
What should you do?

You are lost without a whistle, and no one comes when you call. There is lots of snow on the ground. You hear an airplane flying low overhead. There is a clearing in the woods where a plane can see you. What should you do?

What to Do When Lost

Listen: Remember–never go into woods without permission from your parents or a responsible adult. If, however, you do get lost, follow these steps until help comes.

1. **STOP!** Once you think you are lost, stay in one place.

2. **THINK!** Try not to be afraid. Can you follow your footsteps back to where you started? Are there any landmarks you remember?

3. **LOOK!** What did you bring with you, either in your backpack or in your pockets? What is around you? Is there a hill you can climb to see better? What about shelter? Look for places under leafy trees, by boulders or in fallen or hollow trees.

4. **DECIDE!** How can you use the things you have with you? Decide the kind of shelter you will use and how you can make it more comfortable. If it is very hot, cold or if it's getting dark, make the shelter as soon as you can. Decide what you will drink and eat and how often (you don't want to drink and eat everything right away). Choose a place to make a signal–a big X laid out on the ground where a low-flying airplane or helicopter can see it. What will you make it out of? Green branches, strips of cloth or footprints stamped in snow are all good ideas.

5. **WAIT!** Stay where you are until help arrives.

Directions for Puppets: Cut out the "campers" on the next page and color. Glue the puppet to a craft stick. Practice the poem as a choral reading.

Safety Poem

Use this poem as a fingerplay with young children or as a choral reading/puppet skit with older children. The cut-out puppets can be fun with either activity.

Trees and flowers fill the wood
Making the campsite very good,
But if you wander off alone,
These five rules will get you home!
Stop and think, don't run free,
Look around, most carefully,
Wait for a rescue, folks will come,
Decide to be safe, everyone!

Name _____

My Camping Trip

Now it's time to plan a camping trip or hike with your family. With your parent's help, fill out this camping plan sheet so you'll be all ready!

1. When shall we go? _____

2. Where shall we go? _____

3. How long shall we stay? _____

4. If camping, where will we stay? (Tent, lodge, motor home, etc.)

   _____

5. What will the weather be like? _____

   _____

6. What clothes shall we take? _____

   _____

7. What kind of food will we eat? How much should we bring? _____

   _____

8. What shall I keep in my own backpack? (Remember to keep it with you!)

   _____

9. If I don't have a backpack, what will I keep in a pocket at all times?

   _____

10. Before going into the woods, I will always ask my parents for _____

   _____

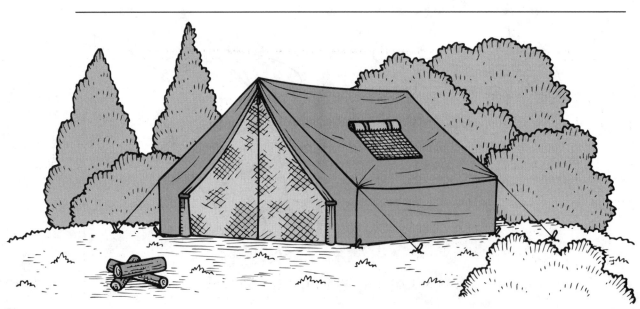

Camping Backpack

Pretend you are Ashley going camping in the woods with your family. She plans to keep a backpack with her at all times. What should Ashley put in her backpack that would help her if she got lost? Look at the pictures below. Cut out each item that she should bring and glue it to her backpack.

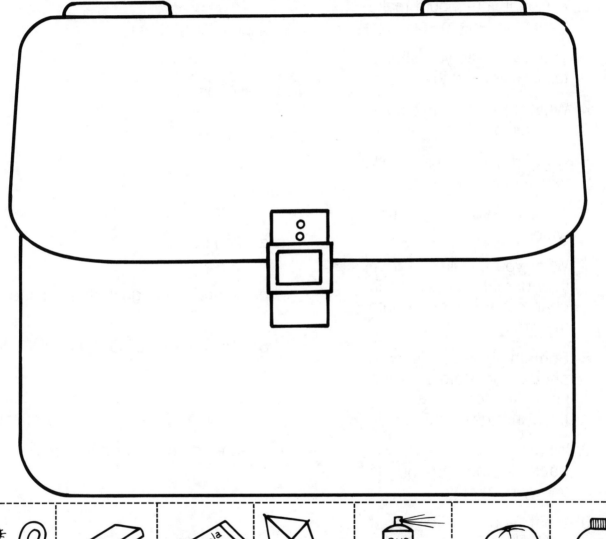

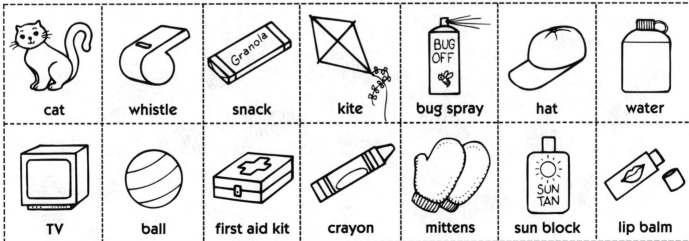

| cat | whistle | snack | kite | bug spray | hat | water |
| TV | ball | first aid kit | crayon | mittens | sun block | lip balm |

Lost: Woods

Checkpoint

Matchup for Safety

Directions: As you read each item, draw a line to the appropriate word or phrase.

1. A good place to find shelter

2. A signal you should make for an airplane to see

3. The five steps you should follow if you get lost

4. What you *shouldn't* do if you get lost

5. A good thing to have with you if you get lost

6. A place you might find water

7. What you should get from your parents or the adult in charge before you go into the woods

8. Something you should check for before using your shelter or walking through brush

9. What you could follow back if the ground is snowy or muddy

10. What you should eat if you're lost

a. permission

b. a whistle

c. footprints

d. your canteen

e. snakes

f. a fallen tree

g. panic and cry or go further into the woods

h. STOP! THINK! LOOK! DECIDE! WAIT!

i. An *X*

j. dried food from your backpack

Chapter 6

The Lake

Feeling Safe Around the Water

Note to Teachers: Water safety is a critical issue with young children. After car accidents, more children die in water-related accidents than anything else. Emphasize water safety around swimming pools, hot tubs, ponds, deep ditches and even amusement park rides that use water.

Maria and Luisa were eager to get to their grandparents cabin. Every summer, the twins spent two weeks there enjoying the woods and small blue lake. Grandma and Grandpa always made sure there was something new to do. This summer they would learn how to paddle Grandpa's new canoe. What fun they would have!

The Lake

As the family drove up the gravel driveway, Grandma and Grandpa came out of the cabin to greet them.

"Where is the new canoe?" the girls asked.

"Just a minute," Grandpa said with a chuckle. "You need to unpack."

"I was planning to have lunch first," said Grandma.

The twins frowned at each other. This was going to take forever.

Quickly they unpacked, put on their swimsuits and sat down to eat the sandwiches Grandma had made.

"Is it okay for Maria and me to go look at the canoe now?" asked Luisa, as soon as they had finished their sandwiches.

Her parents looked at Grandpa.
"Well," he said slowly, "I still need to get the life

jackets out of the closet and into the canoe, so we can't take a ride just yet . . . , but I guess if you both promise to look and not touch the canoe, it's okay."

"We promise," the girls said, as they rushed out the cabin door.

"Let's hurry before they change their minds," Luisa said, giggling. They raced down the path to the lake and ran onto the small dock. Tied up to a piling was the prettiest red canoe they had ever seen.

"Oh, isn't it lovely?" said Maria.

"It is so small," Luisa said, quietly. "Why, I bet I could paddle it without anyone even showing me how," she said, as she swung her legs over the side of the dock and climbed into the canoe.

"Luisa," gasped Maria. "You promised to only look."

"I am only looking," Luisa said. "I am just looking up close."

Suddenly the rope holding the canoe to the dock began to loosen. The canoe drifted away from the dock.

"Maria!" Luisa shouted. "The canoe is taking me for a ride by itself. There is a paddle on the other end. I'm going to get it," she said, as she stood up and began to walk toward the front of the canoe.

With her second step, the canoe tipped over. Luisa fell into the water.

"Help!" she cried. "I can't swim very well. Help me, Maria."

The Lake

Maria started to cry. "Oh, Luisa," she said. "I don't know what to do."

"What's going on down here?" called Grandpa, coming down the path.

"Luisa is in trouble," Maria said.

Grandpa ran to the dock. Luisa was thrashing wildly in the water.

"Luisa," he yelled, "grab onto the canoe."

Luisa reached her arms out and felt the canoe. She held on to it.

"Go get your parents," Grandpa said to Maria. She ran up the path towards the cabin.

"Hold on, Luisa," he called. "I can't swim out for you, but I'll get you. Don't worry." He looked around the dock and saw a long pole. He reached out with the pole towards Luisa. "Grab the pole and I will pull you in," he said.

Luisa tried to reach the pole, but she had drift-

ed too far away.

Just then, Luisa's mother came racing down the path. She dove into the water and swam rapidly to Luisa. Holding her in the special way she had learned as a lifeguard, she swam back to the dock. Luisa's father knelt on the dock, pulled Luisa up and then her mother. Luisa was wet, cold and frightened. Grandma wrapped her in a warm towel and led her back to the cabin.

"If only I hadn't let you go down alone," said Grandpa, shaking his head.

"I'm sorry," Luisa said. "I knew I shouldn't get into the canoe, but I did anyway." She snuggled close to her mother. "I was so afraid. I thought it would be fun."

"Using a canoe can be fun," her father said, "but only if you follow the rules and know what to do. Otherwise playing around water and boats can be very dangerous."

"Yes," agreed Luisa, "very dangerous."

After-the-Story Discussion Prompts

Open with: "Why is it so much fun to be in or around the water?"

- Accept all responses.
- Use chart paper to make a list of ways that we enjoy water for recreational purposes.
- Use chart paper to make a list of all the bodies of water that we might be around.
- Don't forget to include lakes, streams, rivers, the ocean, ponds, swimming pools, hot tubs, large drainage ditches (for catching tadpoles or crayfish) and amusement park rides that contain water (water slides and "lazy rivers" at resorts).

1. The water is lots of fun, cool and refreshing, but can you tell me how the twins, Maria and Luisa, got into trouble at the lake?

   - They went into a canoe without an adult.
   - They did not wear life preservers around the water.
   - They did not know how to swim well.

82

2. What could the girls have done differently, to be safe around the water?

- Stay with an adult
- Wear a life jacket or PFD (personal flotation device)
- Stay away from the water and canoe
- Use a pole or life preserver
- Learn how to swim

3. Why did the girls' mother use a "special technique" to rescue Luisa?

- A lifesaving technique allows you to rescue someone without the victim pulling you under as well
- Lifesaving techniques should only be used by those who have special training
- Invite a Red Cross volunteer to come in and show a film about lifesaving or water safety. Preview the film to make sure that it is not too frightening for your young students.

4. If you do not have special lifesaving training, how can you help someone who is in the water? Think of what the twins' grandfather did to help.

- Use something that floats to help them
- Throw them a rope
- Push a long stick or pole out to them
- **Never go in the water yourself!**

5. All of those answers are good. Do you know that life jackets have a fancy, special name? A life jacket is called a PFD.

- Write on the board:
    Personal
    Flotation
    Device

Define each word and assist the children in understanding how critical a PFD can be in water safety.

6. Why would it be a good idea for the twins in the story, and for all of you, to wear a PFD anytime you are *near* deep water or near a boat?

- Accidents happen quickly and you might not have time to put on your PFD.
- Storms can come up when you are out in a boat, and you need to be ready.
- You might fall in the water.

7. Speaking of storms, can anyone tell me why storms near the water are especially dangerous? Can the rainwater drown you?

- No, lightning is the dangerous issue at the lake or beach. Instruct children to seek cover on the shore (not under a tree) or to crouch down in a boat, when lightning storms arise.

The Lake

Vocabulary

Key Vocabulary

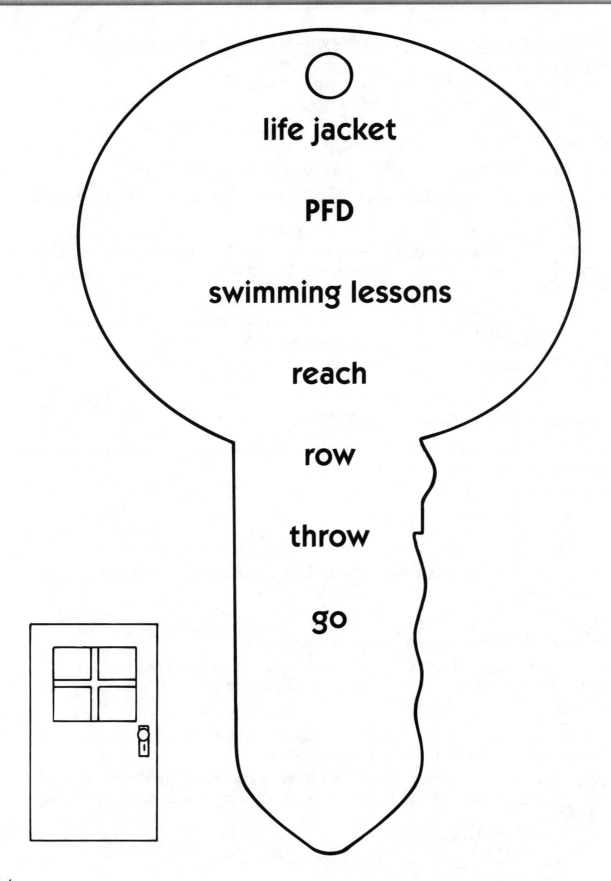

life jacket

PFD

swimming lessons

reach

row

throw

go

Water Safety

Directions: Unscramble the words written on the life preservers. Write the unscrambled words inside the life preservers.

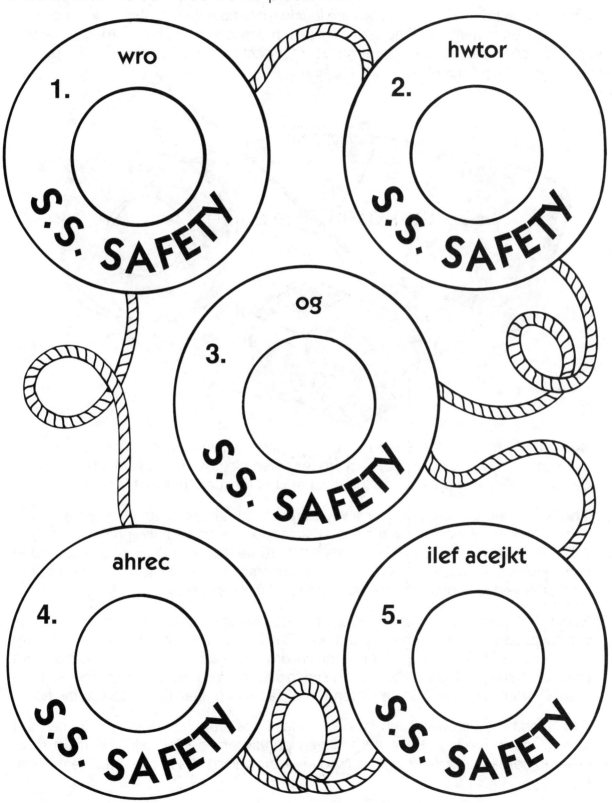

1. wro

2. hwtor

3. og

4. ahrec

5. ilef acejkt

The Lake

Activity

Reach, Throw, Row and Go

Directions: Bring in props: life preserver, Styrofoam™ cooler, plastic soda bottle, fishing rod, life jackets Practice *saying* and *doing* the four steps to water safety.

If someone is in trouble in water, there are four ways to help them to land. Describe and demonstrate each method. Emphasize that each one is to be done in order. If the first method doesn't work, try the next. It is also important to talk reassuringly to the person in the water. Have students practice together.

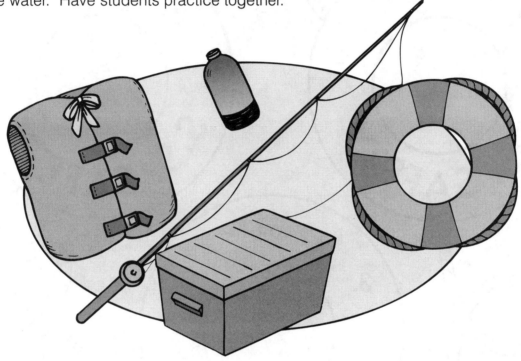

1. **Reach!** Try to reach the person in trouble. Lay down and stretch out an arm or anything you can hold onto–poles, belts, ropes, even clothes. Have students take turns being the person in trouble and the rescuer. Let rescuers pull victims in safely.

2. **Throw!** If the person is too far away to reach, try throwing something that floats. Always look for something with a line attached to it, such as a life preserver, so you can pull in the person. Other things that float are life jackets, plastic beach floats and toys, even picnic coolers! Have student rescuers throw a plastic beach ring with a rope attached to another student and then pull them to safety.

3. **Row!** If there is nothing to throw, or the person is still too far away, look for something you can lay on and paddle out on. Plastic rafts and Styrofoam™ boards are good choices. For young children, or children who are not strong swimmers, it's probably better to skip this step and go on to step 4. You may still want them to practice this step, however, using a pretend "raft" (a towel or blanket spread on the floor).

4. **Go!** If nothing else works, go for help (unless you are a very strong swimmer and have lifesaving skills). Have the children practice going for help. Remind them never to go into the water to help someone. A drowning person can drag them down, too!

86

Water Rescue!

Color the picture.

The Lake

Activity

Water Safety Cube

Directions: Read the water safety rules below and color the pictures. Cut the shape out. Fold along the dotted lines. Glue or tape each tab to the inside of the cube.

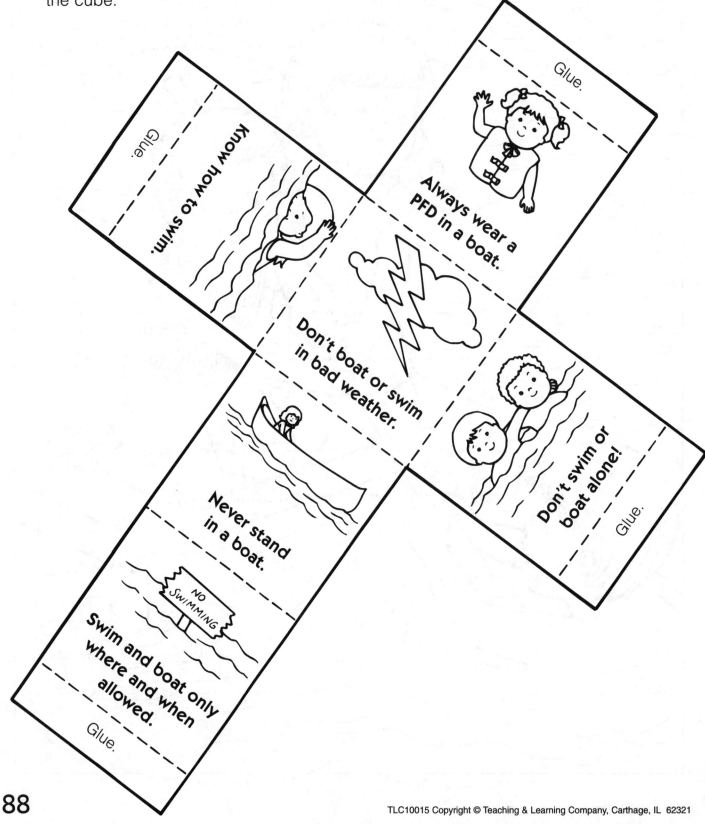

Life Savers!

A life jacket is a type of Personal Flotation Device (PFD). A PFD can help save your life if you fall in the water. It can help you float on the water for a long time. On the life jacket below, list the four ways to help someone who is in trouble in the water. Color the picture of the life jacket (most are bright orange). Place this PFD on the class bulletin board and take it home when you can tell the four rules for water safety–reach, throw, row and go.

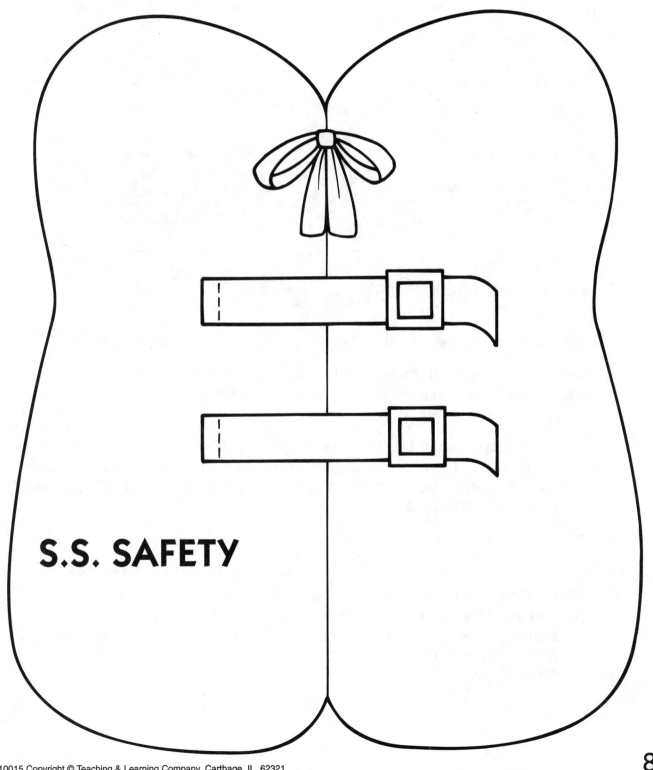

S.S. SAFETY

Water Safety Rules

Swimming and boating can be lots of fun. They can also be very dangerous! Read and study the rules below to help keep you safe around water.

1. Always wear a PFD (such as a life jacket or vest) when you ride in a boat. A PFD should also be worn by people who cannot swim whenever they are near water.

2. Never go near water alone. Always go with someone else.

3. Swim or boat only in areas where it is allowed.

4. Swim only in supervised places.

5. Stop swimming when you get tired.

6. Never swim during an electrical storm.

7. Don't overload a boat. It may sink.

8. Don't stand up or sit on the edge of a boat. It may tip over. Always try to sit near the center. If you must move in a boat, crouch down and hold on to the sides and move slowly.

9. If you're in a boat and it tips over, try to stay with the boat until help comes. Don't try to swim. The shore is farther away than it looks, and an overturned boat is a lot easier to spot than a person in the water once help does come. Stay calm–you'll float better.

10. Learn how to swim.

11. If you're on land and someone in the water needs help, remember to:
    a. **Reach**–try to pull them in with something you can hold on to.
    b. **Throw**–toss them something that they can hang on to.
    c. **Row**–paddle out to them on a raft of some kind (but only if you're a strong swimmer).
    d. **Go**–get help!

Planning a Boating Trip

Directions: Pretend you are going boating, swimming or both. Have your parents help make plans.

1. Where shall we go? _____

2. Who's invited? _____

3. What day shall we go? _____

4. How long will we stay? _____

5. How will we get there? _____

6. What do we need to take with us? _____

_____

_____

7. What do we already have? What do we need to get? _____

_____

_____

8. What special equipment do we need? Where can we get it? _____

_____

_____

9. What rules do we need to remember once we're there? _____

_____

_____

10. What are some fun things we can do once we're there? _____

_____

_____

My Water Safety Book

Directions: Fill in each of the scenes below with pictures of children showing ways to feel safe around the water. Cut out each of the picture strips to make a booklet. Design a cover for your booklet.

What to wear in or around a boat or canoe

What to do if a friend falls into the water

What to do if a lightning storm comes up when you are at the lake or pool

Packing the boat for water safety

Reaching for something while you are in a boat

Taking a baby sister or brother around the water

Riding in a paddle boat or water ride at the amusement park

The Lake

Checkpoint

Water Safety Check

Directions: Mark each statement with *T* for true or *F* for false.

_____ 1. It's okay to swim during a storm.

_____ 2. Never go swimming alone.

_____ 3. Fit as many people as you can into a boat. After all, the more the merrier!

_____ 4. *PFD* stands for Personal Flotation Device.

_____ 5. A life jacket can help you float in the water.

_____ 6. Only swim or boat in designated places.

_____ 7. If you're in a boat and you need something, it's okay to stand up and get it!

_____ 8. When swimming, it's important to have someone (like a life-guard) watch you.

_____ 9. If the boat tips over and you fall in the water, swim as fast as you can for shore.

_____ 10. It's okay to get upset and cry when you're in water and you can't swim.

_____ 11. Always sit on the edge of a boat. It's a lot more fun!

_____ 12. If you're on land and you see someone having trouble in the water–reach, throw, row and go!

Chapter 7

The New Bike

Feeling Safe on a Bicycle, Scooter or Skates

Note to Teachers: Riding a bicycle is one of childhood's great accomplishments. It is healthy and fun! However, to be safety smart, youngsters need to understand how to ride, scoot and skate with a few simple rules in mind. Though the title of this story is "The New Bike," the safety practices extend to scooters and skates. It is helpful to note that accidents related to roller blades seem to be the fastest growing "play-related" childhood accident.

Sasha woke up feeling excited and happy. Today was her seventh birthday, and her cousins and best friends would arrive in a few hours for a birthday celebration. But first, there was her birthday breakfast.

Sasha put on her favorite shorts, T-shirt and sneakers and dashed into the kitchen. Her dad was flipping pancakes. "Pancakes! For my birthday! Hooray!" shouted Sasha.

The New Bike

"What? Is today somebody's birthday?" her dad joked.

"Don't pay him any mind, Sugar Bear," said Sasha's mother. "Sugar Bear" was Sasha's special name. The family sat down to eat Dad's pecan pancakes. Sasha's big sister, Chantal, blurted out, "Can we tell her?"

"What? Tell me!" exclaimed Sasha.

"Finish your pancakes and milk," said Dad, "and we'll go outside and see the surprise."

In a few minutes, only crumbs and some sticky syrup remained. Sasha and her family went outside. There was her new bike. It was bigger than her old blue bike and had no training wheels. The fenders gleamed shiny purple, her favorite color, and the seat had a glittery pink cover. It was a beautiful bike. Sasha said, "Thank you, Mommy and Daddy. I love it! I want to ride it right away."

"Not quite yet," said Dad. "We need to get a few things straight."

"That's right, Sugar Bear," added Sasha's mom. "You need to try on this bigger helmet."

"And here's my present," said Chantal. She handed her sister a gift which held a new set of elbow and knee pads. "Wear these every time you ride that new purple bike," said Chantal, "and every time you pull out on your scooter."

"The same goes for your skates," put in Dad. "More kids get hurt on skates than almost anything else."

"That's right," said Chantal. "Remember my bad cut? It took six stitches to fix that knee, and I wouldn't have needed any if I'd been wearing knee pads!"

"Helmet, knee pads and elbow pads," sang out Sasha. "I'm ready to roll!"

She pulled on her safety gear and climbed on the new purple bike. Dad turned on the video camera to record the first ride, and Mom got her camera set to snap a picture for Granny. Chantal stood ready to help.

The New Bike

"Anything hurt?" said her Dad.

"Is my bike hurt?" asked Sasha. "Just as long as my new bike is fine, so am I!"

"Damage report . . . zero," said Chantal.

"Damage report on Sugar Bear is zero, too," added her mom. "Now do you see why all the safety gear is worth it?"

Sasha nodded. It *was* worth it.

"Start out slow," warned Chantal. But Sasha picked up speed and zoomed down the sidewalk. "Watch out for the . . . ."

Boom! Crash! Sasha flew down the steep curb and off her new bike. Fortunately, no cars were nearby, as Sasha and her bike tumbled onto the pavement.

"I said 'watch out for the curb,' but you were flying like a purple bird on that bike," said Chantal, as she picked up the bike. Mom and Dad were busy inspecting Sasha for cuts and scrapes.

"Are you okay, Sugar Bear?" asked her Mom.

After-the-Story Discussion Prompts

Open with: "How many of you like to ride bicycles, scooters or skates?"

- Accept all responses.
- This is a good opportunity for "personalization." Tell how you enjoy biking or skating now, or perhaps when you were a child.

1. How did Sasha feel about getting a new bike for her birthday?

   - Excited, happy, pleased

2. Why did her dad say, "We need to get a few things straight," before she could try the bike out?

   - To review the safety rules
   - To try on her safety gear

3. Can you name the three important pieces of safety gear that you need while riding a bike or scooter or skating?

   - Helmet, knee pads, elbow pads

98

4. Do you think that any one piece of safety gear is more important than the others?

   - The helmet is critical. A head injury is life threatening. Always wear a helmet.

5. The helmet is the most important thing, because your brain is inside your skull, and it is very delicate. Helmets protect your head. In a fall, it is likely that you will hit your head on something, like part of your bike, the curb or even a tree or fire hydrant.

6. Does anyone have a baby sister or brother who rides in a special seat on back of mom and dad's bike? Why is it so important for the baby to wear a helmet?

   - The baby cannot protect itself in a fall.
   - A baby's head is soft and easily hurt.

7. In the story, Sasha has a small accident. Who can tell me about that?

   - Accept all responses.

8. There are three important bike riding rules, and these rules go for scooters or skates as well. Are you ready? Here they are: STOP! LOOK! LISTEN!

9. Which rules did Sasha discover in her accident?

   - Stop! She did not slow down and stop at the curb.
   - Look! She was not paying attention to the curb that was in front of her.
   - Listen! She did not listen to her sister's warning.

10. That's right. Sasha missed all three rules, and she crashed her new bike. Fortunately, she was wearing safety gear. Can anyone predict what might have happened to Sasha if she had not had her gear on?

    - She might have hit her head.
    - She might have cut her knee or elbow.
    - She might have gotten bad scrapes.

11. Why are the rules STOP, LOOK and LISTEN so important while riding a bike, scooter or skates?

    - Use a chart and marker to make a list of as many reasons as you can.
    - Draw on personal experiences shared by the children.

12. Did Sasha learn a lesson in this story? Why or why not? What might she do differently the next time she rides?

    - Invite individual children to respond.
    - Use this question to assess the children's knowledge.

The New Bike

Vocabulary

Key Vocabulary

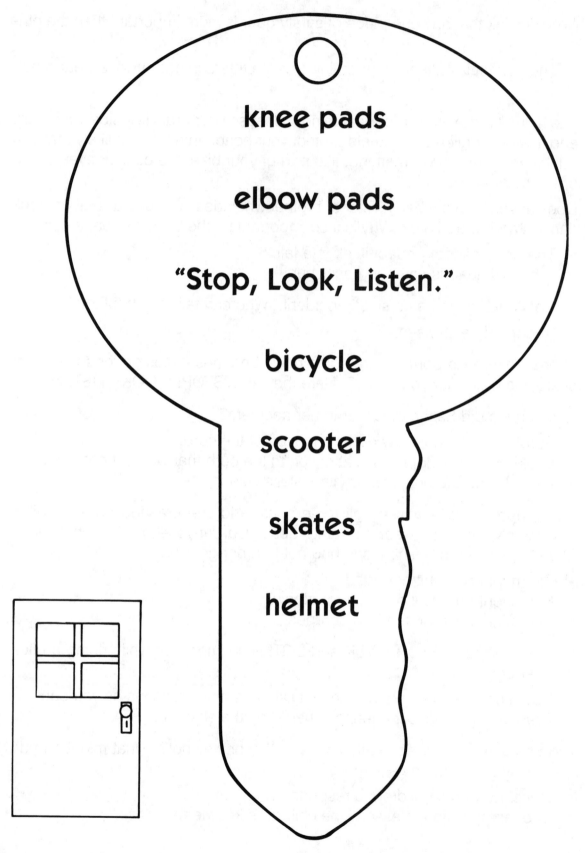

knee pads

elbow pads

"Stop, Look, Listen."

bicycle

scooter

skates

helmet

Name _____

The Wheels on the Bike

Directions: Each of the bikes below has a wheel that is missing. The missing wheel has a key vocabulary word that matches the definition on the other wheel. Read each definition or listen as your teacher reads. Cut out the wheels, and glue the key vocabulary word on the bike with its definition.

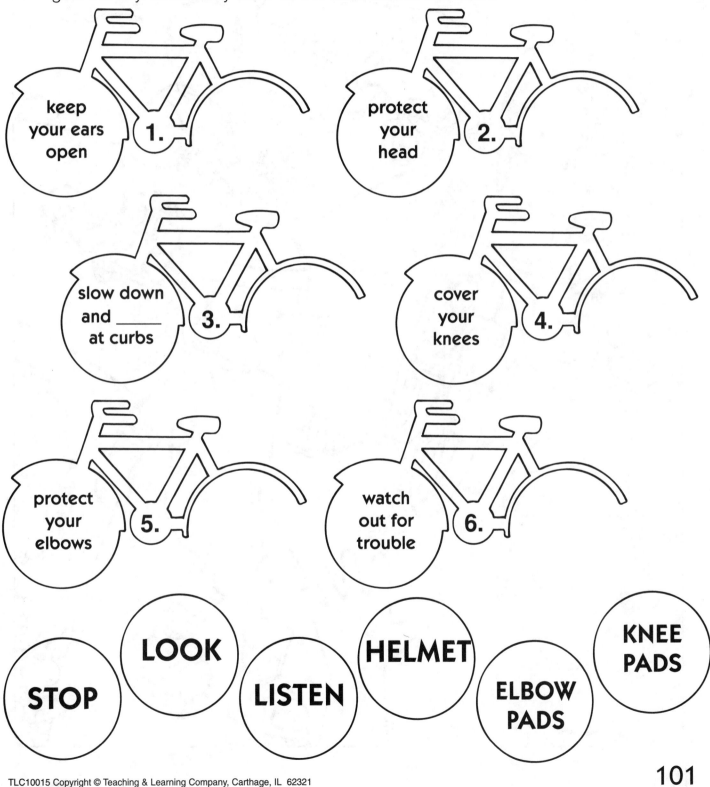

keep your ears open   1.

protect your head   2.

slow down and ____ at curbs   3.

cover your knees   4.

protect your elbows   5.

watch out for trouble   6.

STOP

LOOK

LISTEN

HELMET

ELBOW PADS

KNEE PADS

Safety on Bikes, Scooters and Skates

Color the picture.

TLC10015 Copyright © Teaching & Learning Company, Carthage, IL 62321

Can You Imagine the Perfect Bike?

Directions: Create the perfect bike, with speed and safety in mind. Draw your perfect bike below. Color it. On the lines below, make a list of the safety features.

Safety Smart Bike by: _____
(your name)

_____

_____

_____

_____

Name _____

The New Bike

Activity

Which One?

Directions: Each child should color and cut out the scooter, bicycle and skates on the next three pages. For fine motor practice:

- use brads to attach the wheels to the bike and scooter
- punch out holes to lace on the skates
- decorate the items with glitter, markers, stickers, etc.

When the scooter, bicycle and skates are decorated and ready, children should place all three on the desk or floor in front of them, and listen carefully as you ready the following prompts aloud. Children must decide which one *or ones* of the items you are talking about. This is a critical thinking activity.

1. Loose Velcro™ or laces may cause a fall. You'll fasten these carefully and stand up tall. (skates)
2. Wear a helmet on your head or end up hurt and sick in bed. (all three)
3. Handle bars should be tight or a bad fall will give you a fright. (scooter and bike)
4. Baby sisters like to go, but they need a helmet, don't you know. (bike)
5. Stop, Look and Listen are the rules. Pay attention. Don't be fools! (all three)
6. There may not be a seat to ride, but wear your shoes or stay inside! (scooter)
7. Watch for traffic as you ride; slow down at curbs; never glide. (scooter and bike)
8. Never wear these in the shop or the manager will surely stop! (skates)

104

Name _____

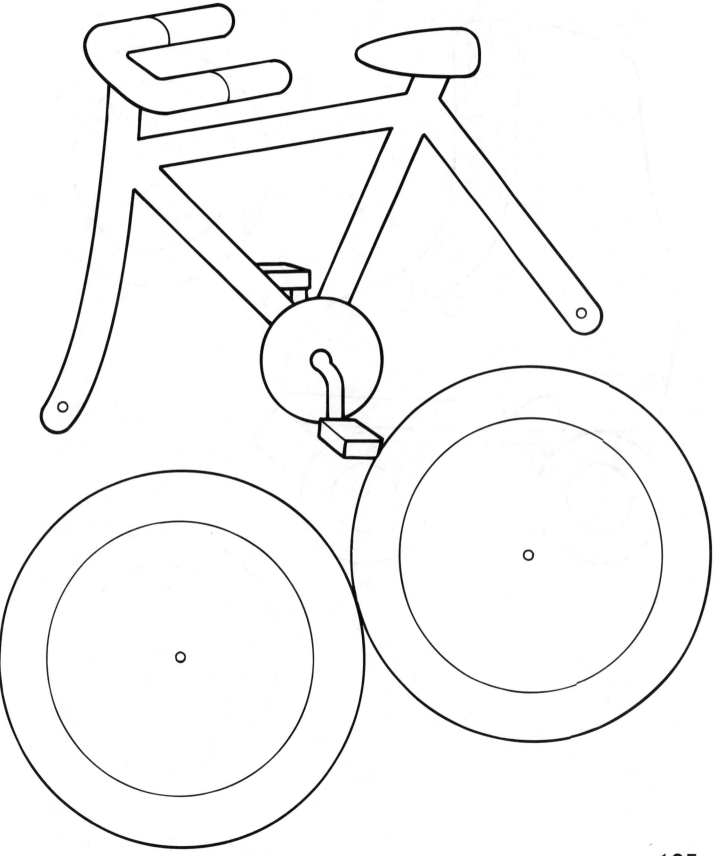

Name _____

The New Bike

Activity

Which One?

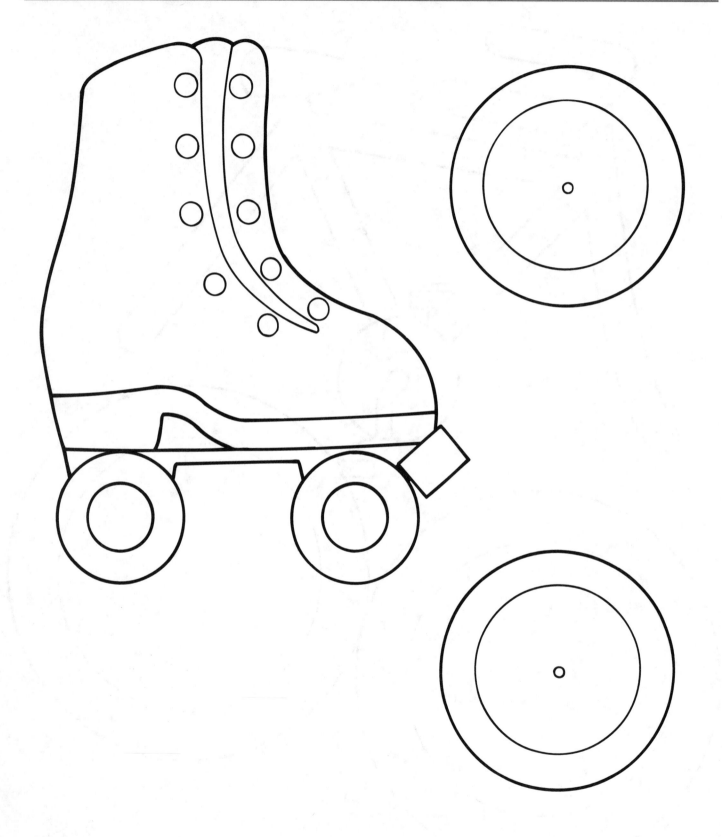

106

TLC10015 Copyright © Teaching & Learning Company, Carthage, IL 62321

Which One?

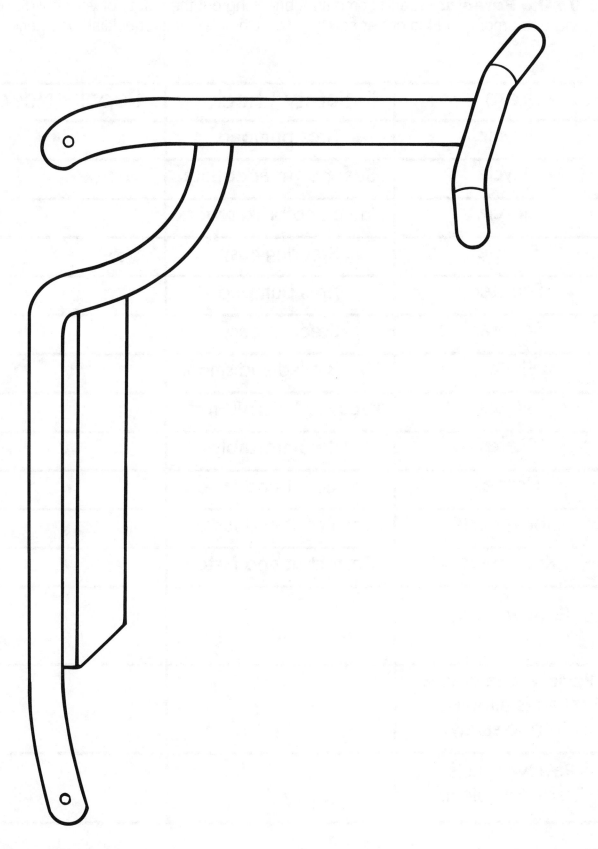

Name _____

Bicycle Safety Check

To the Parents: Spend some time checking out the safety of your child's riding equipment and his or her safety gear. Complete this checklist together.

Item	Safety Check	Repairs Needed
Bicycle	Tires pumped	
Bicycle	Seat height adequate	
Bicycle	Chain and brakes work	
Bicycle	Steering easy	
Scooter	Tires pumped	
Scooter	Steering easy	
Skates	Wheels oiled and smooth	
Skates	Laces or Velcro™ neat	
Skates	Fit comfortably	
Helmet	Correct fit and fasten	
Elbow pads	Correct fit and fasten	
Knee pads	Correct fit and fasten	
Review safety rules		
Review area where child is allowed to ride safely		
Review special traffic problems		

STOP, LOOK and LISTEN!

To the Parents: Create a flip book about the safety smart words: *STOP, LOOK and LISTEN*. You can use a bicycle, scooter or skates in your flip book. Be sure that the child or children in your book are wearing the appropriate safety gear.

Note to Teachers: To make a "flip book," the children design each page, and then place the "biggest page" in the back with subsequently shorter pages in the front. Staple the book at the top, so that when you "flip" it the pictures show. This page and page 110 show the three sizes of pages.

LOOK

LISTEN

110

Name _____

Safe or Not Safe?

Directions: Look at each picture below. Decide whether the child in each picture is following safety smart rules for outdoor play on bicycles, scooters or skates. Circle the pictures that are safety smart. Put an X over the pictures that show children who might get hurt.

1.

2.

3.

4.

5.

6.

7.

8.

Three Stories

Note to Teachers: "Three Stories" about emergencies form the final chapter of *Safety Smart.* By definition these stories may be frightening to young children, so handle them carefully. Emergencies happen. Typically, serious accidents stem from situations beyond a young child's control. Emphasize staying calm and getting help. That is the best way for children to deal with such difficult, stressful times.

Rachel's Story

Julia shook her head. "Please be careful, Rachel. That looks dangerous."

Rachel wiped her sweaty hands on her shirt. "Watch me make this jump," she said. "I've never tried it before."

"Rachel, that's too far," Julia cried. But it was too late. Rachel's hands slipped off the bars. She fell onto the hard ground.

"My leg," she moaned. "It hurts so bad."

Julia bent over her friend. "Don't move, Rachel," she said, "I'm going to get help."

Rachel moaned again. "My leg, my leg."

"I can climb higher than you," Rachel said, as she pulled herself up higher and higher on the monkey bars.

Julia looked up at her. "I think that's too high, Rachel. Please come down," she begged.

Rachel laughed. "I do this all the time. Watch me jump." She jumped from one bar to another, then another.

José's Story

José watched his father carefully saw the piece of wood. Soon they would have the pieces needed to make the new doghouse. José liked to watch his father work with tools and wood in the garage. Dad says I can help him hammer nails this time, too, he thought.

Another piece of wood was lined up on the saw. "José," his father said, "please get me that measuring stick by the wall. I need to measure all the pieces again when I am done."

José could not find the measuring stick. "Where, Dad?" he asked.

His father turned his head to look at José. A look of pain crossed his face, and he yelled over the sound of the saw. "Yow . . .ee . . .ee." He turned off the saw and tried to pull away.

"José," he cried, "I've cut my fingers badly. My sleeve is caught in the blade."

José ran toward the door. "Don't worry, Dad," he said, "I'll get a cloth to put over your hand, and then I will call 911."

"I shouldn't have taken my eyes off of the saw," his father said.

Jennifer's Story

"Time to pick up Daddy," Jennifer's mother called. "Get your raincoats. It is raining hard."

Jennifer and her little brother, Cole, put on their coats and shoes and piled into the back seat of the car.

"All set?" Mother asked, slipping behind the wheel.

The rain beat down hard on the car as they drove down the slippery road. Jennifer had brought one of Cole's small cars to play with. "That's my car," cried Cole when he saw it.

"So what," Jennifer replied.

"Give it to me," he shouted, reaching for it.

"Stop fighting," their mother said impatiently. "How can I drive with all this noise?"

Jennifer stuck her tongue out at her brother. "Try to get it, cry baby," she laughed, holding the car over her head.

"Give it back," Cole yelled, kicking his legs.

"Give it to him, Jennifer," their mother said. Jennifer laughed again. Cole was really getting mad. How funny he looked.

"Mom," he cried, "she won't give it to me."

Mother turned around and reached back angrily for the toy. The car swerved off the road. Jennifer and Cole screamed. The car crashed into a tree.

All Jennifer could hear was the sound of rain on the car roof and Cole crying.

"Mom," Jennifer said, leaning over the seat. Their mother lay slumped against the steering wheel. She did not answer.

"Cole," whispered Jennifer, "I think Mom is hurt. What will we do?"

They looked out at the dark night and heard raindrops on the roof. They were very afraid.

Key Vocabulary

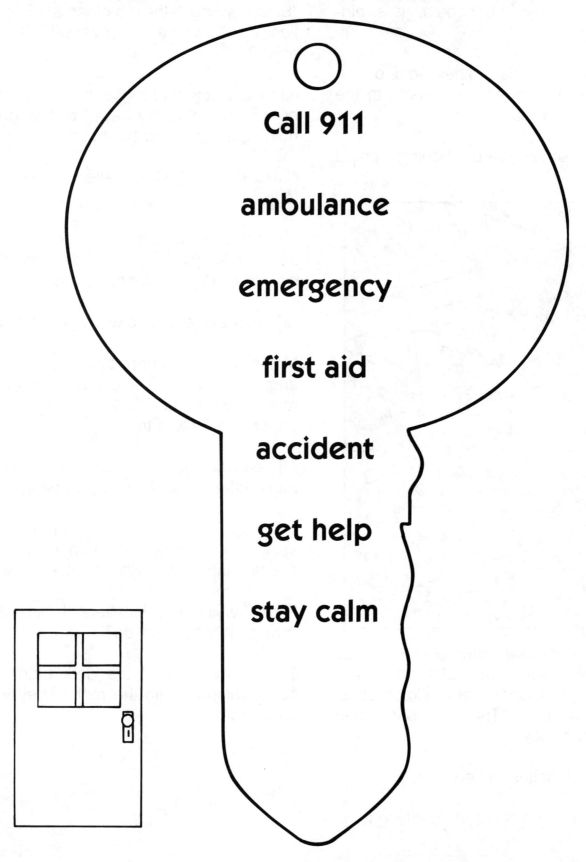

Call 911

ambulance

emergency

first aid

accident

get help

stay calm

Band Aid Words

Directions: Read each of the sentences, or listen as your teacher reads them aloud. The sentences are written on the first aid kits below. Cut out the band aids. Glue each band aid vocabulary word on the lid of the correct first aid kit. Color your pictures.

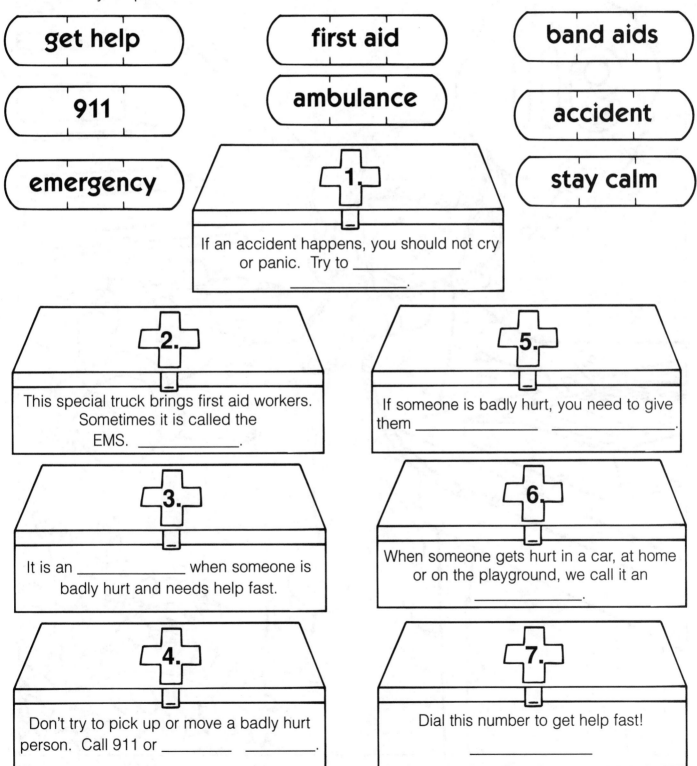

get help

911

emergency

first aid

ambulance

band aids

accident

stay calm

1.
If an accident happens, you should not cry or panic. Try to _____
_____.

2.
This special truck brings first aid workers. Sometimes it is called the EMS. _____.

5.
If someone is badly hurt, you need to give them _____ _____.

3.
It is an _____ when someone is badly hurt and needs help fast.

6.
When someone gets hurt in a car, at home or on the playground, we call it an
_____.

4.
Don't try to pick up or move a badly hurt person. Call 911 or _____ _____.

7.
Dial this number to get help fast!
_____.

Three Stories

Activity

Call 911

Color the picture.

Three Stories

Activity

Help in a Hurry!

Directions: A man is hurt in a car accident. The ambulance is on the way. Find the path and trace it with a crayon.

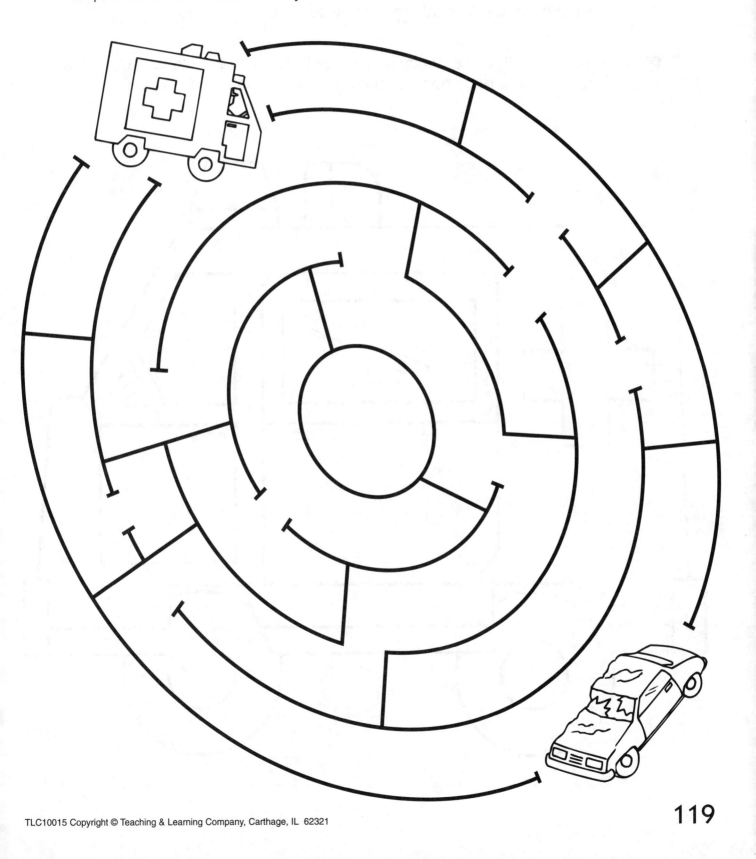

Three Stories

Activity

Help Is on the Way!

Whenever someone is badly hurt, it is an emergency! If you have the 911 service in your area, call that number. If 911 is not available call 0 or the police, fire department, ambulance or local emergency service.

Directions: Write the emergency phone number on the ambulance. Color the ambulance. Take this page home and put it by your telephone.

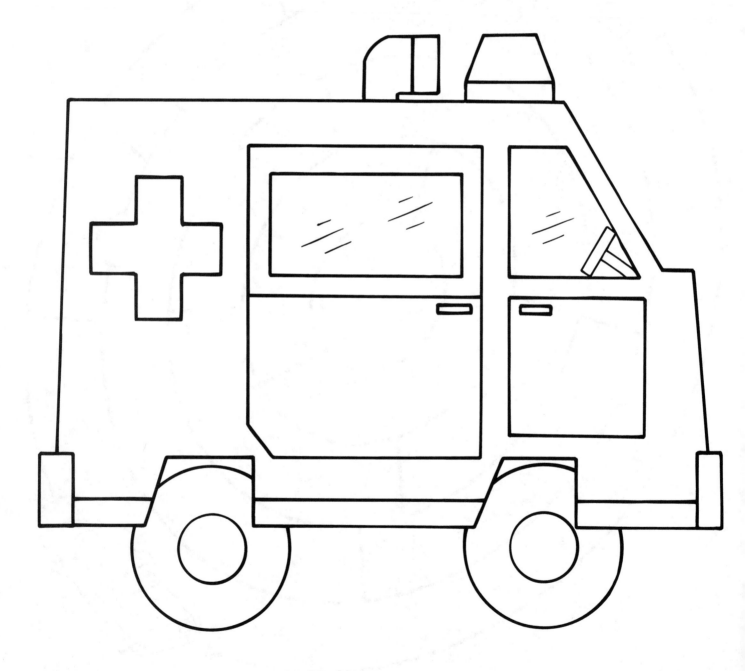

Name _____

Safety Wheel

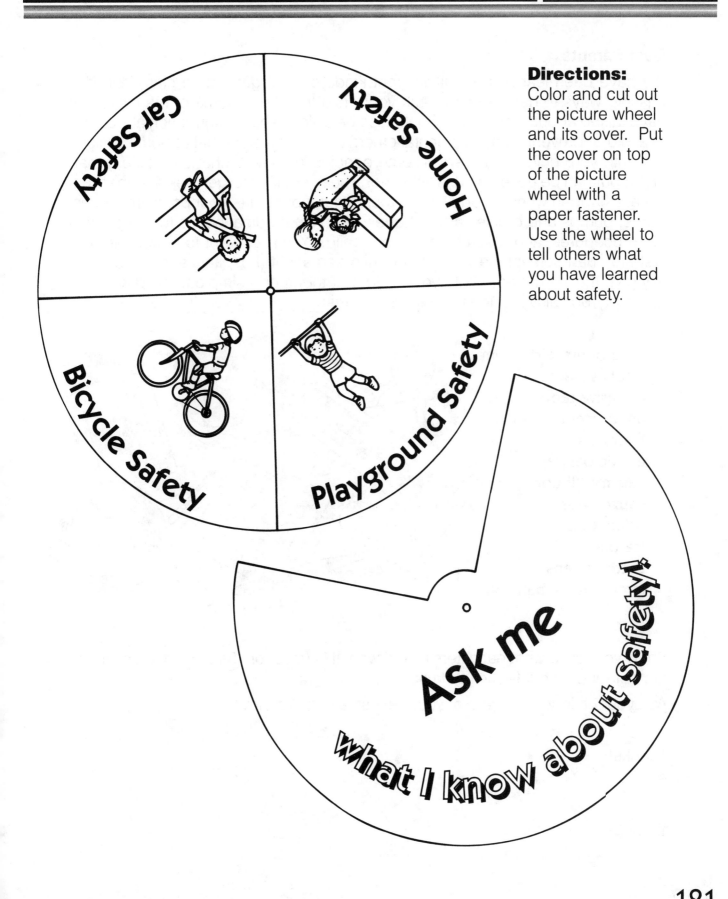

Directions:
Color and cut out the picture wheel and its cover. Put the cover on top of the picture wheel with a paper fastener. Use the wheel to tell others what you have learned about safety.

Name _____

Emergencies Big and Small

Dear Parents,

We have been learning about different kinds of emergencies in class and discussing ways to handle them. Ask your child to tell you some of the things we have talked about. Your child should also be able to share information about how to avoid or prevent many accidental emergencies. As a special at-home project, talk with your child about "small" emergencies–accidents that aren't life threatening but can be upsetting to a little one. These small emergencies are ones that usually happen when an adult isn't around–cuts, puncture wounds, animal bites, burns, bumps and bruises are just a few. Look in medical books for simple first aid procedures, and teach them to your child. You may want to post a pictorial first aid chart someplace where your child can see it (hospitals and clinics usually give these out free). With your child, put together a simple first aid kit. Use an empty box and include the following items:

tube of first aid cream
safety scissors
adhesive tape
antibacterial soap
tweezers
elastic bandages
calamine lotion
gauze pads
safety pins
ice bag
cotton swabs
large, square bandage

Show your child what each item is and what it is used for. Stress that these items are not for play but for first aid use only.

Ask your child to take care of your next small emergency.

Thanks!

Teacher

122

In Case of an Emergency . . .

You have learned many ways to avoid accidents, but sometimes accidents will happen anyway. Here are some things you can do to help.

1. Stay calm. It's hard for someone to understand what you are saying if you are crying or screaming.

2. Don't hurt yourself trying to get help for others. If you are in a car accident, try to get out of the car as soon as possible, but be careful how you get out. Watch for broken glass and sharp metal. Watch for cars going by.

3. Tell an adult. Your family and neighbors are always willing to help in an emergency. Ask police or firefighters for help.

4. If someone is hurt, use the telephone and call 911*. Tell them about the problem. You will also need to tell them your name and where you are. They may ask you to describe the injured person. They may even ask you to do some simple first aid.

5. If the hurt person is awake, try to say things to make them feel better. Let them know that help is on the way.

6. Once help comes, try to stay out of the way. Unless you are needed, it's better to let the emergency people do their job as quickly as they can.

This set of tasks is truly authentic, in that we are looking for performance, not description or explanation. Observe the children as they reenact each emergency scene, and give individual feedback about how to be "safety smart."

You will need the following items:

1. riding car (Little Tikes™ or Playskool™) or box decorated to look like a car
2. plastic tools (saw, hammer)
3. playground equipment (swing, slide)
4. telephone (real but unplugged is best)
5. first aid kit

You will begin by:

1. Setting up three "emergency stations":

   a. the car accident
   b. the tool accident
   c. the playground accident

2. Setting up the "help station" with telephone and first aid kit.

3. Organizing small groups of children to reenact the emergency scenes described on the following page.

4. Assessment: Use a checklist to evaluate each child's ability to:

   a. understand the nature of an accident and emergency
   b. identify sources of help
   c. use the 911 procedure*
   d. explain the importance of getting help and staying calm

*Adapt to your local situation if 911 is not available.

In Case of an Emergency . . .

To the Teacher: Explain to the children that they will be showing you how good they are at handling an emergency situation. Ask them to be creative but to remember the importance of the situation. Each child should select at least two of the three scenes to reenact.

Scene 1: The Car Accident

Using one or more "play cars," children re-create a car accident. They may use a car and bicycle; a collision; or a car hitting a tree, building or pedestrian. The "star" should be responsible for showing how to get help.

Scene 2: The Tool Accident

Using play tools or other "power tool" props, recreate a scene in which someone is hurt by cutting himself. The "star" should be responsible for demonstrating how to handle such an emergency with simple first aid and getting help.

Scene 3: The Playground Accident

Using real playground equipment, the children should pantomime an accident. The focus here should be on getting help and preventing others from getting hurt.

Checklist for Assessment

Name	Car	Tool	Playground	Notes

Name _____

Is It an Emergency?

Directions: You will need a red and a blue crayon to do this page. If the situation is an emergency, circle it in RED. If the situation is not an emergency, circle it in BLUE.

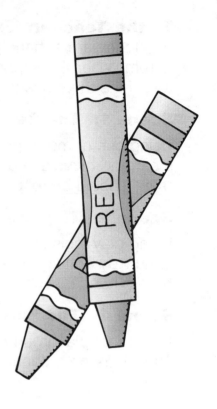

1. You are in a car accident, and your dad is hurt and cannot speak to you.

2. Your sister falls off a swing, and she has a scraped knee.

3. In the kitchen, your mom gets burned by splattering grease and falls down on the floor crying.

4. A car hits your best friend while she is riding her scooter, and her head is bleeding.

5. While you are helping your grandfather around the house, he falls off a ladder and cannot get up.

6. On the playground, a boy falls off the big slide and hits his head.

7. While building a playhouse in the yard, your dad cuts his hand with a power tool. It is bleeding a lot, and he says, "Get help!"

8. While riding to school in the carpool, a car hits your car. Everyone is wearing his seat belt, and nobody is hurt.

Safety Smart Award

For Water, Outdoor, and Car and Bicycle Safety

To: _____

From: _____

Date: _____ Signed: _____

Safety Smart Award

For Personal Body, Substance Abuse and Home Safety

To: _____

From: _____

Date: _____ Signed: _____

Survival Superstar Game

Who will be the first to become a Survival Superstar? Use playing pieces and a die. Roll the die to see how many places to move. Do what the space says to do.

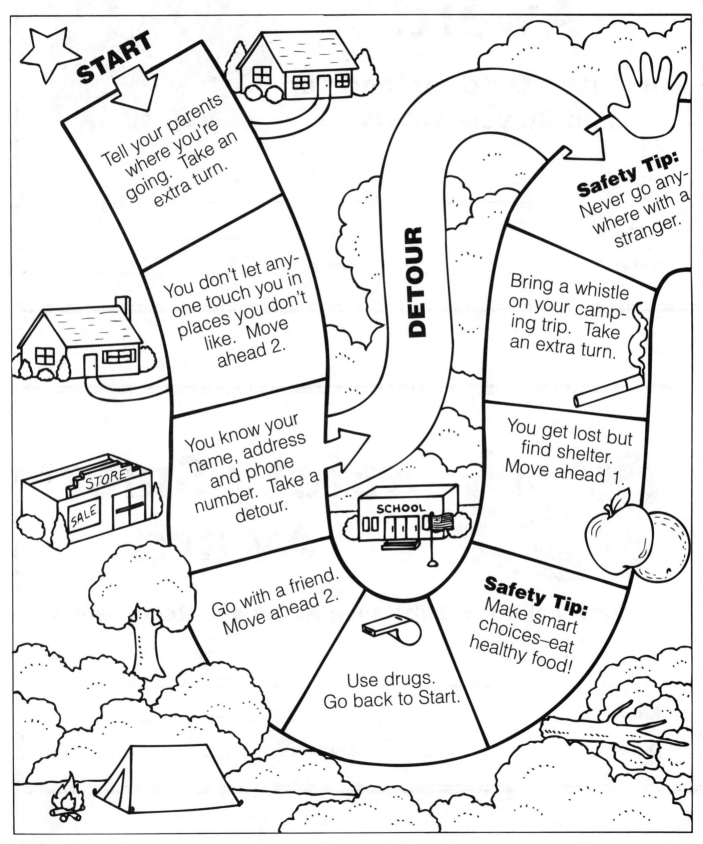

Survival Superstar Game

You tell an adult when someone or something has made you afraid. Take the bridge.

Safety Tip: Never open the door to a stranger.

You tell someone on the phone you're alone. Lose a turn!

You wear a PFD while in a boat. Go ahead 2.

You blew three short blasts on your whistle when you got lost in the woods. Go ahead 1.

BRIDGE

Safety Tip: Wear a bicycle helmet when riding a bike.

You swim where there's a lifeguard on duty. Go ahead 1.

You go up the playground slide the wrong way. Go back 1.

You always wear a seat belt in the car. Go ahead 2.

Safety Tip: Call 911 when there's an emergency!

You leave toys on the floor. Go back 1.

THE END

Answer Key

Lost and Found, page 7

1. home
2. safe
3. stranger
4. neighborhood
5. directions
6. lost
7. strangers
8. directions
9. lost
10. safe
11. neighborhood

A Neighborhood Map, page 8

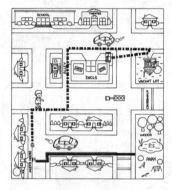

Lost in the Neighborhood, page 14

Underline in green these statements: 1, 4, 5, 6, 8.

Underline in red these statements: 2, 3, 7.

Safety Lock Up!   page 21

1. alone
2. safety checker
3. locked
4. appliances
5. lonely
6. message

Checking the Rules, page 30

These statements should be checked: 1, 3, 5, 7.

These statements should have an X beside them: 2, 4, 6.

Open the Doors to Safety, page 38

1. confused
2. private
3. safe
4. secrets
5. personal
6. touching
7. feeling good

Checking the Rules, page 47

1. no
2. yes
3. no
4. yes
5. yes
6. yes
7. no
8. yes

Healthy Choices, page 55

1. cigarettes
2. drink alcohol
3. clean
4. healthy
5. choices
6. your body

Taking Care of Your Body, page 62

These statements should be checked: 3, 5, 7, 8, 10.

These statements should have an X beside them: 1, 2, 4, 6, 9.

What Happens Next? page 71

Camping Backpack, page 77

These items should be in the back-pack: cat, kite, TV, ball, crayon.

Matchup for Safety, page 78

1. f.
2. i.
3. h.
4. g.
5. b.
6. d.
7. a.
8. e.
9. c.
10. j.

Water Safety, page 85

1. row
2. throw
3. go
4. reach
5. life jacket

Water Safety Check, page 94

1. F
2. T
3. F
4. T
5. T
6. T
7. F
8. T
9. F
10. F
11. F
12. T

The Wheels on the Bike, page 101

1. listen
2. helmet
3. stop
4. knee pads
5. elbow pads
6. look

Safe or Not Safe? page 111

These pictures should have an X over them: 1, 3, 6, 7.

Band Aid Words, page 117

1. stay calm
2. ambulance
3. emergency
4. get help
5. first aid
6. accident
7. 911

Help in a Hurry! page 119

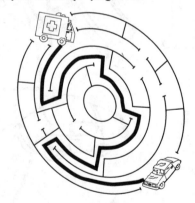

Is It an Emergency? page 126

1. red
2. blue
3. red
4. red
5. red
6. red
7. red
8. blue

130